D1632440

THE LAST DAYS OF SEVASTOPOL

THE LAST DAYS

OF

SEVASTOPOL

By
BORIS VOYETEKHOV

TRANSLATED FROM THE RUSSIAN
By
RALPH PARKER & V. M. GENNE

CASSELL AND COMPANY LTD.
London, Toronto, Melbourne, and Sydney

THIS BOOK IS PRODUCED IN
COMPLETE CONFORMITY WITH THE
AUTHORIZED ECONOMY STANDARDS

First Published in Great Britain, 1943

MADE AND PRINTED IN GREAT BRITAIN
AT THE CHAPEL RIVER PRESS
ANDOVER, HANTS
F./8/43

INTRODUCTION

IN 1939 I went to Paris with one of our sports delegations. The city of Napoleon and Marat enchanted us—the miraculous twilight of Notre Dame, in whose niches the infatuated hunchback Quasimodo still seemed to be hiding, charming narrow alleys, ancient swinging signs, and obscure cafés, the irreproachable straight street prospects opening on to the ampleness of the Champs-Élysées, cut into by age-blackened cornices of sharp-pitched roofs.

I was enchanted by Montmartre, the Latin Quarter, the seclusion of the museums and squares, and by the many remarkable sights of which Parisians had reason to be proud.

While walking through Paris, I recalled palatial Petrograd's triumphant monuments, the new Leningrad's lucid austerity, noisy, crowded Moscow's brilliantly lit evenings, and our national republics' young cities with their original architectural ensembles.

True, after Germany's railroad stations, where even the porters carried revolvers under their aprons, we were shocked by the blatant complacency of Paris, but our undiscerning guides—" French experts "—put down our perplexity to ignorance of the ethnographical peculiarities of France.

Naturally we did not then imagine that in the Government offices of the city monsters were organizing France's terrible betrayal nor did we know the name of the self-sacrificing de Gaulle, who, to save France, was demanding tanks, tanks, tanks; but our intuition was not deceived. Several months afterwards the French capital had fallen and the last resisters had been crucified against the Maginot Line.

Introduction

A little later, in the Carpathians, I had the opportunity to meet a number of western European and Polish intellectuals. They were evacuees. Their coats were stained with the dust of all Europe's roads, their travelling bags were bulging with clothes and souvenirs of ruined homes. They waited in empty mountain hotels for the final frontier delimitation.

We had friendly, sometimes even intimate conversations, though the national political situation in western Ukraine was then most acute and most nervous. They were a mixed lot—experienced actors, journalists, salesmen, racing motorists, doctors, teachers, lawyers, merchants, young scientists, soldiers, obvious adventurers, and unmistakably damnable fifth-columnists. Here were proud, irreconcilable, empty, war-weary people who had lost all national feeling and human dignity. By night, legally or otherwise, some used to cross over the Carpathians to the Germans. Fear had stilled their reason. Others were still uncertain where to go or whom to follow. Many chose us. On narrow Carpathian roads, in dense balmy forests far from Moscow, I then heard for the first time the sad echoes of the war.

The Russian Government did everything to stave off the war, but in a year our land was in flames. The fire spread quickly—considering the precautions, surprisingly so. Gigantic towns in the Ukraine and Byelo-Russia burned like straw huts in the arid steppe. By November the flames were rapaciously licking Muscovy's ancient lands, and scarlet smoke was curling around the walls of the Kremlin. But in these bitter heavy days none of us fled to the borders of China or ran into Afghanistan to wait, as the people waited in the Carpathians, for the tempest to cease. Our whole people rose. A great Russian wall at Volokolamsk and Mozaisk was directed by the inflexible will of the most Russian of all Russians—Stalin—and the Germans were hounded from Moscow.

In the early days of the war our people had to be told what the Nazis were, and with other writers I was asked to describe with hatred the horrible thing that was hanging over our land. On the second day of the war I began to write for the Vakhtangov Theatre the play *Welcome Arms*. Its theme concerned a second European front. While working on it, I recalled my short meeting with the Parisian and Carpathian refugees, and asked myself what these people were doing now, when the war had involved all Europe and Asia; whether they were still marking time at one place and, having once said farewell to arms, were now unable to pick them up again.

The play was written in two months, and then during the period of heavy air raids, when we slept in the theatre, we rehearsed. One night I went home. A bomb hit and destroyed the theatre and until the next afternoon I was thought to have perished. But actually I was already rewriting my burned manuscript from memory. We began to rehearse again elsewhere, but the day before the première was billed, the company was given short notice to evacuate to Omsk in Siberia, for the position in Moscow was becoming critical.

One hundred thousand trains that have become legendary, carrying snow-powdered machinery, moved along the packed railroads of Siberia to the Urals. Millions of dispersed families who had given their best menfolk to the front had been ordered to move far away, eastward. They travelled in freight cars, passenger cars, Moscow metros, suburban trains, flat cars, and in the bitter winter frost arrived at unknown little stations where they put all their effort into unloading gigantic lathes, machines, and heavy factory equipment. Here people who had never known one another before—Kharkovites, Byelo-Russians, Leningrad and Moscow citizens—developed a friendship that was cemented by woe and hatred. Here in the frozen jungles of Siberia they assembled in a period of weeks and months huge plants and factories from scattered machine parts. They worked in an ecstasy of revenge, devilishly. Their hatred found vent in disciplined heroic work.

Old Siberian teamsters, accustomed from time immemorial to driving troikas, began to study internal-combustion engines and calmly awaited spring, when for the first time the virgin soil would be ploughed by tractor.

In one of the most ancient Siberian cities I saw a factory director, a chief engineer, carefully selecting sites for workshops and departments among a cluster of monastery chapels, trying to solve the problem of placing them in such a way as not to disturb worship. It was a difficult, inconvenient, even an extravagant precaution, but the director, though an atheist, took it. Now when the factory exceeds its schedule, the chapel bell is rung.

At Omsk interest in my play suddenly cooled off and it was slipped out of the repertoire. In the director's cold eyes I read his tacit condition: " When there is a second front we will produce the play." There was nothing I could do about a second front, but I did not give up hope for the production and my play was accepted by a small local company. They took quite an opposite point of view. They were afraid they would not finish rehearsing before the second front was opened.

The spirit of the Siberian Ural people responded warmly to scenes in which anti-Fascists hounded the Germans from their country and in which the Czech professor, who was talking on his underground radio finished his speech with the words: "Long live Jean Christophe with a revolver in his hands!" The audience, eagerly awaiting the time when such things will happen, not on the stage but in occupied lands, liked the play and I felt that my persistency had been rewarded, for here in a small theatre in distant Siberia, the Russian people demonstrated a broad internationalism of spirit. Nevertheless, the play was unfortunate. Only Omsk and Sverdlovsk accepted it. Perhaps it was not good enough; perhaps all the other directors decided to await the second front.

On my train journey from Omsk to Sverdlovsk I was telling my troubles to a Red Fleet sailor with whom I was sharing a berth. Probably to calm me, he said: "If you want a subject, come to Sevastopol." The idea seemed promising and I started to work on it at once. A month later I left a building which was guarded by Marines on one of Moscow's boulevards, with documents authorizing me as a playwright and a special correspondent of *Pravda* to travel to the Sevastopol garrison and attach myself to the Black Sea Squadron. In those spring days when, by an order of the High Command, Kerch was abandoned, I flew to Sevastopol and entered the last Crimean stronghold, whose eight months of siege had already given it legendary glory.

I had the luck to be in the hell of the last days of Sevastopol's heroic defence, personally to see, hear, and survive happenings which surpassed in valour, bravery, and endurance anything my imagination could picture.

If my impressions of those sacred days can somehow be helpful to British, French, Czechs, Poles, and all those others with whom we talked about the future through the night in Paris and the Carpathians, then I shall be more than satisfied and happy.

LIST OF MAPS

CHAPTER I

THE BLACK SEA port where ships went to and from
Sevastopol is famous for oil, borsht, fish, and flowers as
bright as paint. Its flowers have an irritatingly sharp
scent. One could use them in borsht instead of pepper.

And naturally here were women ; among them many
were beautiful. But all were busy—busy with the war.
With southern vitality and verve, every day they were
releasing more and more men for the front. They were
working everywhere, these women—dark, fair, young,
old, coquettish, plain. They looked after shops, cut hair,
shaved troops, and checked trains in and out. They
worked on the new coastal defences, administered the
town's affairs, helped to pump oil into tankers, unloaded
urgently needed trainloads of munitions, and guarded
the quays. I saw one gay young commissary officer at
the harbour gates, challenged by a girl whose flaming
red hair streamed over the flowing sailor collar of her
overalls, stand ten minutes while pretending to look for
a pass. He was trying to make it as long as possible
in order to find out her home address. But it was not
long before she placed a whistle between her unimpeach-
able white teeth and summoned the guard. At that
moment the officer found his " lost " pass and retired
hurriedly.

The next day we saw the girl kneeling beside an anti-
aircraft gun crew firing her rifle at a German reconnaissance plane. In fact, the town had been captured
by stern, beautiful women. Sailors, arriving, called it
the " matriarchal capital." Their menfolk, who had
been called up for service, were not all far away. On
the outskirts of the town, in mountain ravines and led

1

by experienced commanders who had been released from hospitals, they were passing through a stern military school. In full fighting kit, under the stentorian commands of their persistent lieutenants, they dashed into the attack, bumped down on their bellies on sharp stones, or crept hundreds of yards forward, scraping their skin until it bled. They rose in bayonet charges, splashed through a stream, put machine guns in position, built pontoons, and dragged half-submerged tanks from mud and clay. All day they strove against an imaginary enemy, storming a bright-blue newspaper kiosk representing a German pillbox. Under such training the weak became strong, the strong herculean.

At dusk these men and women met on beaches, and hundreds of nude bodies, separated by natural modesty and military discipline, plunged into the water. Snorting noisily, the infantrymen washed away the dust and sweat of the day's training while the women swam far out to sea, refreshing themselves before sleep. Later in the evening, scarred ships arrived from Sevastopol smelling of scorched paint, charred timber, and war.

Hundreds of women waited on the pier. With bunches of onions and garlic, the favourite dainties of people coming from Sevastopol, they met their husbands, alive or dead. They shed tears of joy or of despair, stood silent beside their dead or wept on the breasts of the living. The sailors crunched the crisp onions between their teeth, putting the garlic in their pockets for the long journey back. Gentle hands smoothed the beloved heads of wives.

Yet among all their sorrow and joy there was a false note, too. Some of the girls were simulating joy too obviously as they greeted their husbands, who either saw and understood, or saw and were bewildered. The

2

understanding ones returned these greetings curtly, handed over their pay, bade a quick farewell, and coldly returned to their ship. Others, unbelievingly, fussed clumsily for a while around their powdered wives, bringing smiles to the faces of the girls' lovers. There were no fights. The people in this war were disciplined even in such delicate matters. But in the eyes of their husbands these women read a threat, and when they had said farewell, they turned to their lovers, anxious for the future.

Then the ships turned about, loaded with things without which the war cannot continue, and with people to use them.

The dead were covered with overcoats and were borne home. All night someone sits beside them watching their closed eyes, and at dawn they are taken to a crowded cemetery. Then their widows return to work as another day begins, full of tension, difficulty, anxiety, and waiting for more ships.

At this particular port a submarine commander told me the following love story:

" All this happened," he said, " on the way back to Sevastopol. It is a funny thing, but I have noticed that the oddest things happen to me on my return voyages. When I am outward bound, no matter how risky the job, nothing ever happens. That is why I am not afraid of death, because I know for certain that on my way to the other world something amusing will happen to me.

" As you know, I am very inquisitive and I am ready to give up my fifty-four years of life for a good anecdote. Well, this all happened two months ago when I was still a helmsman, my captain being my best friend. We had done some good military business off Constanza and were ready to submerge and head straight for Sevastopol. When we plunged, leaving our periscope above the water,

3

something absolutely devilish happened, just as in Gogol's story *Han Küchelgarten*. (By the way, I read that story again. It is perfectly written.) Just imagine, in the middle of the day the horizon disappeared. Just disappeared! But that was not all. The periscope registered a hell of a black night. Then, in a second, the horizon appeared again and it was daylight, and then in a few seconds it changed from day to night and back five or six times. Consider, too, that the weather was ideal— no storm or mist.

"Well, we supposed that some kind of rag had stuck to the lens of the periscope and we dived a little deeper so that the waves could wash it away. No good! Still the same alternation—day and night. You can imagine, we were absolutely at the end of our wits. Then one of the sailors asked the captain if he could look through the periscope. He watched intently and then said: 'He is talking.' 'Who?' asked the captain. 'The man,' he replied. 'There is a man outside asking us to surface.' When we had risen enough, we learned that one of our crew had been trapped on top of the conning tower when we had submerged and had been hanging on to the periscope, trying to flash to us in Morse signals by putting his hand over the lens. The captain embraced him for ingenuity and gave him five days for slackness. Don't you think it was a rare experience?" asked the commander.

I agreed, but asked what it had to do with his promised love story.

"A lot," the captain replied, enjoying my bewilderment. "From there the whole story begins. We took the sailor on board and submerged again thinking that would be all for the day. About two hours later in the evening, to give the men some air, the captain thought it safe to surface. And up we popped plumb into the

4

centre of an enemy convoy. Two heavy oil tankers, plunging heavily, were slowly making their way to Odessa. Their escort of Rumanian minelayers and German E-boats were in a lazy, scattered formation, as if bored by their slow-moving charge. We weren't noticed and put a torpedo right into the minelayer on the left. She was up in the air in a few seconds. Then we put another into the biggest tanker's belly. We saw her crack in two, with oil pouring from her, and sink in a few minutes. Then, reserving our last torpedo, we drew near to the starboard of the second of the tankers and plastered her from bow to stern with all our heavy machine guns and our two cannon. I don't think that a single shot missed its mark—just on the water line. Twice we raked her length and literally sawed her thin rust-worn hull. In five minutes water was pouring in. The ship listed to the stern and began to sink slowly. Burning oil on the surface of the water masked us from a destroyer whose disorderly firing threw all of the other vessels of the convoy into panic. They began to whine and hoot, trying to save themselves from the destroyer's fire.

" Then, from behind the sinking tanker, the destroyer swooped down upon us, determined to ram us. We plunged—five fathoms would be enough for safety. There was a sudden shock, so strong that we thought it was an explosion, but no, we were intact though no longer sinking. The gauges registered ten fathoms, yet we had stopped sinking. Who would have believed it? We had struck shallow water. We thought, maybe we had better surface and fight our way to Sevastopol. Not a chance. Maybe it would be better to turn under water and head towards the sea, but then our engines would betray us. The captain decided to switch off the engines. There

5

were several seconds of silence, tense and nerve-racking. Then there came suddenly a deafening crash, another and another. The lights went out; everything was vibrating like a top. Those were the first depth charges. Then they began to burst all around. At any moment we knew we might be squeezed between the caving-in walls of the submarine.

" Do you know what depth charges are? They are much more powerful than high-explosive bombs, just because the explosion shifts water and not air. Well, the submarine was out of control. She was being bumped about on the bottom like a log. Then there were some minutes of silence, with our nerves straining to the cracking-point.

" From a tilted tank water dropped steadily on the metal floor. It was unbearable. We imagined that the noise would give our position away. Somebody crept to the tank and held a finger over the tap. Then the explosions started again. Sloops and cutters were combing the sea for us. They were dropping charges systematically, covering one square and then going over the sector again diagonally. But somehow or other we kept alive, thanks to good luck and the flexibility of the casing of the submarine. We squatted round a small lantern, holding our breath and listening to that devilish din outside.

" The enemy, I suppose, not seeing traces of us on the surface, imagined that we had perished by diving too deep. Anyway, after a while two E-boats began to drag for us with steel cables. The cables, which scraped along the bottom, caught in our radio antenna and then slid along the sides of the submarine. Now the Germans knew just where we were and how deep. We then heard the metal boots of a diver clanging as he stepped over

6

us. Every step echoed in our hearts. Most of us knew we were for it. The diver scrambled up our conning tower and hammered angrily with a metal bar. We knew this meant an invitation to surrender. Some time passed, then something, we didn't know what, scraped along outside and bumped heavily on the bottom. It was a steel net. It was very quiet now. The enemy knew we couldn't move in any case, and that our death was certain. Someone moaned. We had to tie him up. Our air would not last much longer. Men began to get that blue look about them.

" From his place the captain rose as if everything were perfectly normal. He approached a little table on which a domino board was set, and facing the crew he said: ' Let's play.' No one said a word. ' Come on,' the captain repeated.

" The commissar joined him, but nobody else moved, and then for a third time, but authoritatively this time, the captain said: ' I definitely challenge my Number One and my Gunnery Officer to play a hand of goat '—that is the game we usually play.

" All four took their places and began to play. ' Double six,' the captain said; ' that means we must surface. There is no point in waiting.'

" Turning to the crew, the captain said: ' All right, if we've got to die, at least let's do it in a decent depth of water.'

" We surfaced slowly, and down the open hatch fresh sea air poured. Alongside our last torpedo the gunner waited for the captain's order to blow us all up and send us back to our ancestors. Singly, with our fingers on our tommy-gun triggers and taking grenades or machine-gun drums by hand, we clambered to the deck.

" It was dark and still. No ship was near. Nothing

but small buoys on the edge of the trap flashing the International signal: 'Enemy submarine located.' But E-boats and a ship with a jumbo crane were coming towards us from the coast. We could see the phosphorescent surf breaking against them. The Germans wanted to hoist us up and capture us intact.

"As they came nearer and nearer, we tore our hands and broke our fingers in getting clear of that net. Then at full speed we smashed our way through it and headed for Sevastopol.

"What do you say to that story? Pretty rare, isn't it? I should say unique."

"Yes," I said, "it is a fine tale, but where does love come in?"

The captain excused himself for a moment to read a cable that had been handed to him. Meanwhile the commissar, who had joined us and who knew the captain's ways well, whispered: "If you want the captain to tell you his story about love, you will have to ask him to tell you one about his own bravery." Which I did. "At your service," the captain replied, and he then began his new tale.

"It was a great love, a rather strange love, and sometimes hard to understand. There were two men in the story. One was the captain, the same fine fellow I have just been telling you about, and the other was his mate. One, the captain, was very ugly and rather bent, with a pockmarked face and sad eyes. The other—well, he was just the opposite. I am not a good story-teller and can't describe him any better than that. Well, let us say that he looked every inch a guardsman.

"The captain's name was Maxim, the mate's Oleg. Both were from the Northern Squadron, where they were known and liked. They both loved the same

8

woman, but she loved only one of them, and both of them knew it. Naturally they were jealous, and their jealousy would make them go about their work in a silent, concentrated way. There was room for love as well as bravery in their lives.

" Whatever port we put into, we used to see waiting on the quay the familiar woman's figure with a shawl drawn around her shoulders. We always knew it was she who was waiting. I don't yet understand how she found out where we were going to arrive. But there she was, at Novorossiisk, Batum, Poti, or wherever our submarine called.

" I have never seen her close up, but from afar she gave an impression of being a rather sad and reflective type. When the captain went ashore she used to approach him slowly and take his arm, and when we were in our home port she would take him with her into town.

" The mate used to go ashore much later to sit on a mole from where he could see the submarine as well as the house. Sometimes he waited there till dawn. Sometimes we would get urgent sailing orders, and then on a signal from our vessel he would go up to the little white house with convolvulus clinging to its front, carefully knock with his pipe on its closed wooden shutter, stand aside a little, and wait for the captain to come out. When he did they would hurry in silence to the submarine and silently put out to sea. The woman never saw them off. She only came to meet them.

" A month ago, as she was leaving Streletz Harbour, there was an explosion in the submarine, caused by escaping gas. The mate and I by a strange chance were not killed. We could see the captain, smeared with blood. All his force was spent when he lifted his clasped

9

hands, and as he went down he waved to us. We knew it was farewell.

"The mate, who was badly wounded himself and was only just able to cling to a spar, hoisted himself from the water and cried out to the sinking captain: 'Maxim, Maxim, I won't touch her.'

"That is the whole story, the love story. The survivors were given a new submarine. The mate became captain. I was the mate. We went on taking fuel and shells to Sevastopol, bringing back wounded, women and children. A short while ago the new captain got homesick for the north and was transferred to Murmansk, where, they say, he has been sinking the Germans all right. That is all. Well, good-bye. Now we have got to go back—to Sevastopol."

We bade one another a warm farewell. While waiting for the submarine to sail I was wondering whether to write all this, and asked myself what it all had to do with Sevastopol. Everything, I decided. Sevastopol was surrounded—and surrounded, too, were cities which she loved and which loved her. This port where I met the captain was part of the "Big Land" for the sake of which the people of Sevastopol fought so long and desperately. Sevastopol, too, owes much to the stubborn heroic people of those little mainland towns and ports, and all the glory and all that happens there or on the way there have directly to do with Sevastopol's glory and valour.

As the submarine left I shouted good wishes for a lucky voyage to its crew. Beside me stood a woman with a shawl drawn round her shoulders. I recognized her by her sad face.

CHAPTER II

SOON we should be landing. Later we would have to drive along the highway which crossed the mountain range to Novorossiisk. I knew that our flight was nearly over, not because of what the map showed, but because our junior pilot began to lay out well-pressed suits and glossy shoes. One by one, taking one another's post in turn, members of the crew climbed out of overalls, washed, shaved, put on uniforms, and took their places again at the controls, the maps, or the radio. Naval pilots do not like to land on " the coast " untidy, especially as " the coast " has so many young Cossack women.

We were dropping sharply, circling twice. From the plane into a farmyard below, a small package fell. Somebody picked it up, unrolled it, and then waved a welcome. The package contained the latest Moscow newspapers, a bottle of eau-de-Cologne, a pair of big galoshes, and a copy of the magazine *Crocodile*—the eau-de-Cologne for his sister, the galoshes for his mother, and the papers for his father. That is the way the burly, shaggy-headed fellow who handles the overloaded plane so easily lets the family know about himself. Last time his father received a new lens for his spectacles and Crimean geranium seeds. The geraniums were probably blossoming already, or perhaps only just ready to.

Sometimes he would throw only a letter. A small piece of white paper, glittering, would float slowly earthwards while someone from the farm would pant and puff after it far across the fields. The last one which was opened and read by its receiver, standing alone in the fields, read: " We have been at the Rumanians. Look on the map

11

for Ploesti. We are coming back empty—dropped everything. If I am not moved to another front, I will throw you something on my return flight. No wounded, but we have Andrei, dead, aboard. Don't tell Olga. Let her get used to it. Regards to all, Lyosha."

The rain of presents which came down on the farm soon convinced people of the advantages of aviation over those other branches of the Army in which sons or grandsons were serving. But their envy was short-lived when the Moscow newspapers were handed to the local Soviet whose chairman, in his fine ringing voice, read them aloud to all. He rather enjoyed doing this because the new schoolmistress admired his voice.

Forty minutes later we were landed at an aerodrome near a farm settlement, from which I had to continue by road to Novorossiisk.

It was a place abounding with gardens, beehives, and wheat, with sunflowers, poultry, fruit and much else of an incredible plenty. It was like a green carpet spread at the foot of the Caucasus Mountains. Evening had fallen and somewhere somebody was singing. Could it be that not far away Sevastopol was tossing in agony?

Beside whitewashed, tin-roofed houses, on cottage chairs under cherry trees, were sitting the most beautiful of Russia's women—Kuban Cossacks. With dazzlingly splendid physical perfection, they are a little bit plump, a little bit sleepy. They radiate such irritating tranquillity that they repel you for a moment ; then they make you feel as though you want to dance the trepak and then spend the rest of the night by their sides.

When night came—the cool starlit Kuban night— pilots went into these dark jasmine-scented gardens and till dawn forgot everything, even death that lay behind or before them. For many it was their last taste of a

12

woman's tenderness; the women knew it and were generous.

About twenty years ago, when I was a little boy, I used to play in a farm. Now I remembered some of the strange child-dreams I used to have, and one especially of street cars full of fizzling, bubbling jam. I would howl in my sleep and bring my elders to my bedside with anxious questions. I was still overwhelmed with those memories when I drove next morning along the fine highway to Novorossiisk. From the crest of a pass in the mountains, the Black Sea sprawled below. You could trace its depth by the intensity of its shades of blue-green. The scaly ripples glittered in the sun, and though, where it touched the coast, the water seemed to be black, at the horizon it merged unnoticeably into the white noon sky.

Novorossiisk, the city of cement, with its desperate north-east winds and elevators innumerable, a city of sirens, locomotives, and cranes, this day had a cold, stern look. A few hours before, on the other side of the pass, it had seemed to me that the south had not changed even in war-time. But here, after descending from a car, I saw ships with their delicate lines distorted by zebra-like camouflage patterns, the sad, surly faces of shoe-blacks indifferently drinking their wine, and noticed that the inhabitants had even stopped bathing in the sea. I understood then that the south had changed, even if its heat and flowers remained.

Yes, for today, Novorossiisk was as cold and repellent as a Siberian forest in autumn. War had wiped its smiles away and this city, which was accustomed to go about its work joyfully and light-heartedly, was now tense and angry—angry with the Germans who had shaken its boiling southern temper into a deadly, bloody hatred, angry because of the dead bodies of its first air raid, because of the Ukraine, Byelo-Russia, near-by Crimea, and, above all, because Sevastopol was being pressed against the Black Sea. It was good that these people had become more grim in their mood, for nobody can repay an insult and take revenge more fiercely than the people of southern Russia. Cossack bravery and the spirit of the Black Sea Marines have often torn the enemy to pieces. Here on these concrete piers and asphalt streets there took place the final scenes of the collapse of the White armies. It was here from these torrid shores that remnants of Denikin's* armies piled into overcrowded vessels, and it was in this harbour that by Lenin's order the Black Sea Navy sank its fleet rather than let the Germans take it.

For a long time their masts were visible above the water and reminded all who were passing of the ships below. Shaken by storms, their gaunt shapes swayed; and sailors going by this dead water raised their caps and muttered: " Never mind, we will build new ships." And they were built. In those stern, half-forgotten days this town was as grim and unfriendly as on this morning. What about it? We did not expect to fight the war sitting at a microphone in a comfortable armchair. We knew what it would be like, for we remembered how it was before.

Recently no ships had left for Sevastopol because another port was being used. I did not want to wait doing nothing, and when the chance of going by air was offered, I took it. A few hours later found us in the harbour of a small seaside resort where at that time one of our naval air squadrons was based. In the evening the squadron commander, a man with the irreproachable appearance of an old naval officer, showed me some

* Anton Denikin (b. 1872) was commander-in-chief of the White armies in southern Russia, against the Bolshevists, in 1918.

14

recently developed photographs. We looked at them through a magnifying glass. We saw the fuselage of a plane sinking and two Germans with uplifted hands. As the wings of the plane were already below the water, the men looked as if they were sitting on the water with their arms held high pleading for mercy. That was the result of a battle earlier in the day between one of our bombers and a Nazi reconnaissance plane. " Is that the sort of thing I might see? " I asked. " Possibly," the commander replied.

In the early morning the coast is rather misty. A short way from shore is a two-engined hydroplane, looking as I imagine a whale would if it could smile. A cutter is on the way to the plane, with mechanics to overhaul its engines. We enter a white villa. On its terrace broken pillars lie scattered like skittles, by the blast of a bomb. It used to be a kindergarten. It is now the pilots' club and mess room.

A thin trickle of water is falling on the green cloth of the billiard table, but nobody minds, and a crew just before leaving for a nine-hour reconnaissance flight are finishing their game. White balls are splashing through puddles in the American game of pool. Splutteringly the last ball is pocketed. The navigator has won. He says to his opponent, a commander: " Honourable Captain of the Third Rank, I like direct hits not only on enemy transports but on the billiard table." The joke is well received, and in his notebook the radio operator, who keeps the scores of billiard matches, ships sunk, and witticisms, after a general consultation puts two points against the navigator's name. Accounts will be straightened out after the return from the flight. They were good fellows, those airmen. Were? Do not the dead remain heroes?

15

They never call each other by name. Each has a nickname, private to the group and born from battle friendship and good humour. Among them I remember " Batum," " Double," and " Sign First." Batum was the commander's favourite town. Double had been twice decorated, Sign First was what the second pilot used to say when issuing pay cheques, for he was the crew's bookkeeper. The blue-eyed, blond machine-gunner had been given a girl's name—Verochka.

Verochka was late for breakfast and it was decided to teach him a lesson. The breakfast was concealed and, instead, there was prepared a special dish. A large slice of salt fish—Vobla—soused in honey and garnished with candy, lettuce, and mustard. " What is it called? " asked the surprised Verochka. " Paraguayan beefsteak! " chorused the rest. The machine-gunner carefully lifted the fish on his fork, cleaned it with a piece of bread, and, cursing the cook, began his breakfast. Immediately the real breakfast was produced and the radio operator wrote a point to everybody's credit.

That is the way these men, who fly to meet death every day, behave. One of the most popular of their childish jokes was directed against a representative of the commissariat. He looked after their supplies very badly and bored everybody by always asking for a joy ride. All of the other crews had refused, but this one decided to take him up. They put him inside the bomb cage of an old field bomber, taxied several times round the drome, and then told him that they were at sixteen thousand feet. At that very moment the bomb trap was opened and the passenger dropped two feet. What their human bomb lived through during his fall can be left to the imagination. He made a terrible fuss and the crew got two days' C.B., but since then supplies have arrived punctually.

But these fine lads could do other things than play practical jokes. Each carried a picture of drowning Nazis, and conversations revealed them to be perfect naval pilots.

As soon as we were on board, the float was removed, and circling once over the drome, we headed for the open sea. Ahead of us lay nine hours of scouring the Black Sea, watching the movements and position of enemy transports, and bringing the information back. Back? When I saw the completely changed faces and manner of this light-hearted crew, I began to realize that we might not come back. But it was too late to think that way—one had to keep an immovable face. A gloomy mist met us over the open sea. It stood before us like a dense white wall and was apparently endless. We climbed above it and after a long while flew into the clear as if between snow fields. A little above us were clouds. Perhaps it would be better to turn back? No, the reconnaissance must continue till it is cancelled from shore. This is just the weather through which transports are likely to be threading their way with cargoes. I overhear a dialogue between the pilots: " To the right, up, two Junkers." " I see them. Shall I give the alarm? " " No use." " Why don't they attack us? " " Do you want them to? " " No, but, all the same, why don't they? " " Didn't see us, the fools. For such work I would have taken all their Iron Crosses from them."

I began to sense conflicting feelings, of fear and intense curiosity and satisfaction, and yet regret that they had not noticed us. It would be interesting to be in actual battle with real Germans. I was not actually afraid, but how describe my sensations? How would I have felt if those two big grey bombers had not been swallowed up in the clouds?

" How do you feel? "

" All right," I replied politely, at the same time concealing my mixed emotions. I was ashamed to lie. So all right it was.

We had been a long time over the sea and were now somewhere near Constanza. Far away was the Bulgarian coast. There was no point in going any farther. We turned back. The fog was denser. Our wing was no longer visible. It was foggy inside the plane. I could not even see the control board or the second pilot. What had happened? We were falling seawards into an abyss. The slightest fault in judgment and we would have been dashed into the sea. I looked over the side. Thirty feet from the water we came out of the dive, but we still dropped—to a little more than ten feet. Would we be able to swing clear if suddenly, out of the mist, an enemy ship appeared?

For two hours we flew thus, heading homewards. It was exacting and wearying work for the pilots. At last we climbed to a thousand feet and the mist vanished. It seemed as though we were nearing our base. At that moment the siren rang with its ear-splitting sound. I can still hear its jackal howl from the tail, where the rear gunner had been the first to spot the enemy. It drowned the sound of the engines, warning all that the hour of deadly danger had struck. It was time for battle. The siren persisted so that I longed for the battle to silence it and now realized that my feeling arose not from fear but from having nothing to do among all these active people. Can you remain calm when someone is shooting at you? Can you be indifferent when you are the only one who cannot fight? And here, as later in Sevastopol, I realized that the most unpleasant sensation in the war is to observe.

On our trail, about fifty yards away, flew a light Heinkel bomber. Now I was looking at one in action, not a plane being exhibited in the Theatre Square in Moscow or in a trophy exhibition, but one which was alive and hostile. I was overwhelmed with excitement to see what the enemy would do. Ten minutes elapsed, Though a little nearer now, the Heinkel clung on to us without firing. How long could it last like that? Perhaps he was waiting for the rest of the wing, from which he had been separated in the mist. The sky was now quite clear. The mist belt was far away. We had no chance of making it. We knew that the German plane had every fighting advantage over us; that our reconnaissance hydroplane was seriously outmatched in speed and range by the bomber. That had to be accepted. It was strictly against instructions for us to open the battle. Our task was reconnaissance, not fighting. There was nothing for us to do but wait. I wrote down another dialogue that I overheard:

" Pump out gas vapour from the tank."

" Okay, pump switched on."

I asked why and was told that there was danger of the vapour exploding if we were hit.

" Issue lifebelts."

" Okay."

" Release floats."

Immediately our retractable floats dropped into position. This was to be ready for an emergency landing. A radiogram was sent to shore: " Enemy plane met, forced to engage."

" Okay."

" Correspondent get into the hatchway."

I didn't like that order at all. I moved to the hatchway wondering why. Then I realized that I might have to jump and that this was the best take-off.

19

Batum gave his place to another pilot and, noticeably pale and tensely controlled, he hurried to the machine-gunner, saying: " Vera, don't shoot till he does, but then, by God, let him have it."

" Okay, by God, it will be," replied Verochka, who was crouching behind his gun.

That is all that was said. In those ten minutes of nerve-racking anticipation I realized that despite their efficient and irreproachable bearing, despite all their experience in risking their lives, all their training of will and nerve, each new engagement placed on them a heavier strain.

Since Sevastopol I do not believe people who say you can get used to war. Yes, you can become passive or indifferent through fatigue in a single engagement, but in a daily round of battle, never. The men before me now were not poseurs, briskly mouthing loud slogans and oaths, but just the opposite. These men, who were stirred to the depths of their souls by the urgency of the situation, and were growing pale and tight-lipped, had their eyes fixed on the enemy as keenly and anxiously as in their first experience of battle.

Swift as lightning the Heinkel swung to the right. I saw the black cross on its surface. I saw a burst of fire. I didn't know that you can actually see shells in the air, but they were whizzing under our right wing. I saw them splashing in the water, far below. We were falling sharply in a series of jerks. Fall or manœuvre? " Don't jump," the radio operator shouted; " I will wave when it is necessary." We continued to lose height. We were just in time. A second later and we should have been hit. Above our wing now, between our two motors, more shells were flicking by. The Heinkel was trying to shove us into the sea. He was sure of himself and was ready, probably, to photograph us in our moment of destruction. Losing room to manœuvre, we were an easy target against the surface.

It was not clear what Batum was doing. I had nothing to do but think, and wondered why he was speeding above the water line like a desperate, hunted criminal. The spare pilot quietly said: "You are not lucky to-day, Fritz. You may peck us to death, but it is all right; we will swim our way out"; and pointing to a lifebelt, he asked me whether I knew how to blow it up. I didn't. "All right, we will teach you down there." I didn't like that "there."

For about ten minutes both planes continued to dive, sideslip, and elude each other. Shells and bullets rained into the sea. Now the Heinkel was attempting to swing close to us again. I could hear the sound of its approaching engines piercing me like a drill from head to foot, and could see the odious swastikas on the grey fuselage as it swept over our left wing, keeping out of the range of our machine guns. For another minute nothing happened, but we knew that another fight lay ahead. Batum gave Double his place at the controls for a moment. He ran to the machine-gunner and said: "I am attacking head on. Aim for the cabin. If we go down, it must be both of us." And he went back to his place. On the way he grabbed a cushion to give himself a better position.

For the first time he strapped himself in and Double did the same. I saw them look at each other. It was clear, they had decided not to leave the plane, whatever happened.

Rearing suddenly and steeply, the Heinkel banked and turned into a hurtling dive. Gritting his teeth and hunching his head deeply between his shoulders as if preparing to leap, and with his body trembling in rhythm with his gun, the machine-gunner was crouching unnaturally behind it, shooting fiercely at the enemy as he came into a ferocious dive. Discarded cases which rattled and rang in a metal container spilled out on the turret floor. The gunner shoved them away impatiently with his feet. The Heinkel was still in a dive and was falling directly on us. Was he done? Was he falling? It was too late to swing out of the way, so we dipped and his wing flashed past our nose. We heard one of the machine-gunners shout hoarsely: "Damn him, he is all armour. We need cannon."

Below there were two heavy splashes as two bombs fell. I had not heard of using bombs in air fighting like that. It meant that he had no shells left. Now it was only a battle of machine-gunners' nerves. Good God, Batum was smiling. Wasn't it too early? But then he performed a miracle. With feet and hands he began to make the most monstrous manipulations, with speed and efficiency, playing freely and easily with all sorts of buttons, pedals, and switches on the complicated control board—and all this blindly, for his head was turned to watch the Heinkel beginning a new attack. He opened the throttle, squeezing every ounce out of the engines. We rose. A little higher and we could ram. Yes, ram with one of our floats, for if we won we could get home without floats. Nearer, nearer, and now nearer, it meant victory or death. We could see how our bullets were passing just above the German pilots' leather helmets while others were hitting their armoured wing. A little more, a little more, and then nothing could save the enemy. We had failed. The distance between the planes lengthened as the Heinkel sheered off.

Suddenly we began to fall. Our right motor had

stopped. Tilting, we slipped down and our left motor stopped—we were gliding silently. The radio operator shouted in a desperate voice: "Don't jump. Maybe we can float all right." Watching the Heinkel, I could sense its elation. Now, having put our motors out of commission, his task was easy. He dived on us like a hawk. Then, when it seemed as though everything was over, both our motors roared out. We straightened and went hard into a frontal attack. Batum's bluff had worked not only on the enemy but on us, for we had begun to count our last seconds of life. Now our right float was bearing relentlessly down on the Heinkel, which was less than a hundred yards away. I could see the pilot's face behind the celluloid. Why didn't he look at his kill at such a moment?

Then I noticed that his machine guns had stopped. All sorts of ideas flashed through my mind. Hands up? A dream? Then I realized that some time during those last hectic moments each plane had finished its ammunition, had used up all its fighting power. Snatching an empty water bottle, Verochka flung it angrily in the direction of the Heinkel. His fist was raised and shaken in frustration as the enemy quickly made off. Batum called after them: "Get out of our sea." "Not a particularly witty, but a nice remark. I will give you one point when we get back," said the second pilot.

So our battle ended stupidly. We were soon back at our base. After that, I thought, I was quite ready for Sevastopol.

Next morning, to celebrate our safe return, the mess gave a party to which I was welcomed as a comrade in arms. In addition to me, there were present a bear, a donkey, several peacocks, and two foxes. The big friendly-looking bear ambled across, greeting us with a mumble. With startled ears, the grey donkey stood knee-deep in the sea, sadly and noisily complaining of its saltiness. The shabby peacocks angrily scuttled away from boys who had played havoc with their bright tails. Only the foxes were indifferent, absorbed in dreams of the Caucasus, beside rough models of which they crouched on the terrace.

The party was being given in the courtyard of the regional zoo, which was now boarded up and closed. The curators had given the animals a last meal and had gone to the front. The caretaker, who had got drunk, was drowned in the sea, and the animals were abandoned. Disconsolately they had wandered round the empty settlement, begging for food from the few remaining inhabitants, who were pushing supplies home from the market in perambulators. The donkey, the foxes, and the peacocks used to follow these perambulators and stand unhappily beside house doors. You could see that they did not care for begging, these animals which had been used to being served; but they were hungry, and humiliated themselves. Each evening they returned empty and angry to the courtyard, where a caged bear was dying of hunger. Boys let him out finally, and on a Sunday the bear ambled up the main street and made for the mountains. Three days later he came back to his cage. The old fellow understood that a mountain was no place for one who had lived all his life with human beings.

Batum's crew adopted the animals from the moment it arrived. The crew spanked and drove away the children who had tortured the birds, hired a sober keeper for the bear, fed the animals from their own kitchen, and brought them dainties from the market.

I have never enjoyed myself so much as I did in that cheerful, dignified, witty company of men and animals.

Toast followed toast. We sang songs to the Russian bear, who would tear into pieces any German jackal; drank to the health of the donkey, for whom there had been made a cap from the remains of a German pamphlet raid; and paid our tribute to the wily fox. Besides jokes, much good sense was spoken and sincere things were said. Near the bear cage the animals listened. They kept their eyes on the food, but did not make any demands. They knew that their turn would come. The bear got a bottle of vodka to himself, and taking it in his two paws, he drained it to the last drop. Verochka, by general request, recited a tender poem—" You came to me in a gas mask." Photographs were taken, after a long argument as to who should sit next to the donkey. When night fell, Batum rose and addressed the company with mock solemnity: " Conversations have continued long after midnight in an atmosphere of great cordiality. I ask you, ladies and gentlemen, to take your places for bed." The party bade farewell to the animals and broke up.

Days passed, days when the harbour was in a thick mist and when no plane left for Sevastopol though reconnaissance was continued. Then, while returning one evening, the floats of Batum's plane got caught in some fishing nets in the harbour. All of the crew were drowned.

Their bodies were not found; there was no funeral.

Before I left the place, which had become unbearably hateful, I visited the animals, which were hungry and disconsolate again. Not accustomed at that time to seeing death every minute, I went away with complete indifference about the future, being anxious only to put behind me the unknown graves where heroes had perished so absurdly and needlessly.

CHAPTER III

WITHIN an hour ships were leaving for Sevastopol. Each in turn, and very politely, the captains of the destroyers declined to take me aboard.

The chief of the naval officers had his headquarters in an old warehouse near the harbour gates. I decided to appeal to him.

Entering an office, I saw a man with a deathly livid face streaked with yellow, who stood at a wide-open window, with a far-away look, swaying rhythmically on strong thick legs set wide apart. He was dressed in clean, well-pressed summer whites. His eyes were dull and indifferent.

Through the window you could see the dirty waters of the bay. Rubbish was floating on its surface. Sometimes the hubbub of the port—brief thuds from the loading or unloading of transports—was audible. Then there was stillness again. It was clear that this man had acquired his habit of standing, gazing, and rocking in this way out there on the wharves and not at the office.

" Yes? " said the chief naval officer without turning. I handed him my pass.

He read everything through carefully. " Impossible."

" Why? " I asked, feeling immediately that there was no hope of getting anything from this cold ruthless man.

" You and your documents have arrived too late."

" I don't understand what you mean," I persisted.

" I am sorry," the chief said, and then after a moment of reflection he added : " Visits to Sevastopol have been prohibited since yesterday."

" By whose order? "

26

" The Admiralty's."

" Where is the Admiralty? "

" At Sevastopol."

" Does that mean that there is nobody higher than you at this port? "

" Yes."

" Whom can I appeal to? "

" If you want an immediate reply, only to me."

Saying this, he turned and looked me straight in the eyes. I found it difficult to hold his swollen bloodshot look and said: " It is senseless."

" Who knows? " he replied with faint irony.

I must finish this, I thought and for the last time said firmly: " You *must* let me go. Do you understand? It is your duty to send me to Sevastopol."

The chief drew close to me and asked: " Can you, alone, do the work of five divisions? "

" No," I answered.

" Then you have nothing to do in Sevastopol. But, if you insist—"

" Yes, I insist," I hurriedly broke in, trying to take advantage of his moment of hesitation.

" Well, if you insist," he repeated.

" I do."

" Well then, I must ask you to follow me," and with these words he led me into the next room.

" Come in. This is my home. Introduce yourself. This is my wife." He paused. " This is—Sevastopol! "

In the middle of the room, on its only two chairs, lay a rough open coffin, and in it a woman. Her eyes were open and she seemed strange—not breathing.

The chief naval officer went to a window and poured brandy into two dirty glasses.

" It arrived yesterday," he said in such a tone that it

was difficult to tell whether he referred to the brandy or to his wife's corpse.

"Friends did it for me. Otherwise she would have been buried there. So many doctors have been killed there. One cannot transport every corpse."

Suddenly he turned to me and, gripping a glass in each hand, he brought his lined, tired face close to mine. Tears streamed down his drawn cheeks.

"I should be going, not you, to Sevastopol," he said in a firm voice.

He approached the coffin and, gazing at his wife's young but already slightly darkening face, he said:

"I would have found the sniper that killed her."

The air was heavy in the room and I moved to the window. The chief put his glass on the floor and knelt beside the coffin.

The silence was unbearable and, thinking about the sniper, I asked: "Can one only avenge one's own?"

He pressed his wet cheeks against his wife's hands, rose to his feet, picked up the glass, drank a little, and said: "Isn't she—But isn't she yours?"

We gulped down the rest of the brandy together and returned to the office.

"Within an hour everything must be loaded," he said briskly to a man who rose as we entered. "And, remember, without this cargo Sevastopol cannot fight. It is not eating radishes and fooling round there, you understand."

"I understand," replied the rather jaunty-looking fellow.

"If the job is not done," the chief continued, "it means that you are a scoundrel, and in war-time a scoundrel is shot without waiting for a lawyer's speeches. Is that clear?" ·

" Yes," replied the fellow. " May I report? "

" Well."

" You recommended me for a decoration. Now you are cursing me in front of a civilian."

Here the fellow became embarrassed, and halted.

" I asked for the decoration for whatever was fighting against the scoundrel in you. If it wins, you will get the medal. If the scoundrel wins, you will be shot. That is all."

With a faint smile, the quartermaster left. Apparently he knew and rather enjoyed his chief's strange behaviour.

" Good-bye," said the chief, stretching out his huge raw hand. " By the way, do I smell of drink? "

" No," I said, and left.

A fresh wind rose in the harbour, lightly ruffling the sea. The last of the destroyers, which was turning sharply in a scurry of foam, disappeared behind the lighthouse. Again I thought I had been left behind, thinking of the dead woman with the live eyes, her husband and my own sluggishness.

I reached the mole where the flotilla leader was loading.

" Where are you going? " I asked a sentry.

" To sea," he replied bluntly. " To which shore? "

" Perhaps you would like me to tell you how many bombs we are carrying."

" Don't pester the sentry with questions. Sentries aren't put there for that." I turned to meet an officer of the vessel.

" What are you looking for, comrade? " he asked.

" I hope for Sevastopol," I replied.

" Hope for Sevastopol? " the commander echoed, laughing so heartily that the sentry stiffened to attention. After examining my papers several times and repeating

" Hope for Sevastopol " till we reached the gangway, he said: " Allow me to introduce myself. I am the flotilla leader's commissar."

Leading me on board, he ordered a sentry to find me a cabin.

" Afraid it's rather stuffy," the commissar apologized, " but it doesn't matter ; you will sleep in Sevastopol."

We left almost at once, after a great clanging of bells and telephoning of orders through loud-speakers, the hoisting of bright signal flags, and other apparently chaotic actions. Slowly we pulled away from the mole. The chief naval officer had come to see us off. For a moment I wondered whether he would not jump into the water. Noticing me, he raised his cap and, waving it, shouted: " Lucky journey! Come to see me when you get back." Then, turning as abruptly as in that room, he walked briskly back to his office. His wife was to be buried that evening.

It was rough in the open sea, with a stiff wind. Some-one was playing an accordion. The wind snatched it from the player's hands. It rolled along the deck, where a big wave swept it from sight.

" Serves you right," someone said sarcastically to the Red Army man who had lost the instrument. " Wait till you get a bomb on your napper ; then all your waltzes will jump out of you at once."

" Eh! You fool, when we get to Sevastopol it will be you who will cry out for lack of music," the soldier replied to his grumbling neighbour ; and pulling his over-coat round him, he turned away.

The destroyer was overloaded. It was crammed with things without which Sevastopol could not resist. The decks, the cabins and the hold—every corner—were crowded with boxes, big and small. And on them lay infantrymen, grimy with the war, as close together as in trenches—coat collars turned up, backs to the driving wind and stinging spray. Some who had drunk heavily before leaving, to drown their melancholy at going into an uncertain battle, became dizzy in the strong wind and, resting their heads on machine guns or clasping tommy guns, sprawled on the cases while trying to sleep. Their neighbours covered them with coats and good-naturedly replaced any caps that were carried away by the wind.

Others, who pressed themselves against the warm walls of the engine room or steam pipes, frowned grimly at the stormy, hostile sea.

Swiftly cleaving the waves, the flotilla leader headed straight out to sea. This was her fortieth trip within two months. No ship in the Black Sea Squadron had threaded its way through so many mine fields. Because of her speed she had visited Sevastopol more often than any other vessel. Her adventures were material for the most fantastic, though true tales. The commissar used to say: " It is better to fight the most terrible sea battle than to break through to Sevastopol, in that unequal struggle with scores of bombers and torpedo-carriers.

Add to that the enemy's submarines, E-boats, and widespread mines, and the Battle of Sinope reads like child's play compared with the journey to Sevastopol.

We were making good time—soon Sevastopol. Huge waves broke across the decks, splashing over the cargo and dragging with them the sleeping soldiers. Shaking their drenched overcoats, the men wandered round the ship looking for dry, comfortable quarters. A hundred of them crowded into the corridors, getting in the sailors' way. The alarm siren sounded. Nobody paid any attention to it.

The Last Days

A man in a broad black raglan coat with a bush of stiff whiskers over his full red lips raised his hand and shouted: " Be still, Siberians."

No one heard him. The man in the raglan made his way to a lower control point, took out his revolver, and fired it into the air. " Did you hear that? " he called. Amid the silence that followed, he added: " That is the chairman's bell. Order, please."

The men smiled but their conversation was resumed in a more orderly way.

The man in the raglan replaced his revolver in its leather holster, and, standing on a pile of cases among the Red Army men, addressed them in a loud voice with a Volga accent:

" Honourable infantry: It is my duty to inform you that there is a hell of a storm blowing up. I am telling you in good time because you are dear, precious to the Navy as people going to defend our beautiful wife and friend—white-walled Sevastopol. As soon as the ' business ' begins, such as the shooting of anti-aircraft artillery or bombardment, there is to be no craziness whatsoever. Sailors have to run about, sailors have to shoot, sailors need plenty of room. If in the middle of this arsenal you start fighting, too, the Germans will sink us like fools. These are my orders: First, do not move about. Second, take a rope and tie yourselves up. Tie yourselves firmly so you will not be washed overboard. Third, whatever happens, stay dead still. Keep your limbs under control. Anybody who gets in the way during the battle we will probably throw into the sea. Now lie down and keep still."

" Is it far to Sevastopol? " asked someone.

" Not very far," the captain replied.

" What is it like there, Comrade Commander? Is

Sevastopol on a hill or in a valley? " someone asked from among the infantrymen, who were now lively again.

" On a hill," answered the commander.

" On a hill? That is better. Easier on a hill. It would be more difficult to fight in a valley."

" And which do you like better? When it is difficult or when it is easy? " the captain asked.

All laughed, and someone shouted:

" You are going to take us right on to the Malakhov Kurgan,* aren't you? "

" What is your name? " the captain asked.

" Sizov," answered the Red Army man.

" All right, Sizov; when you leave Sevastopol, there has got to be a Sizov Kurgan right next to the Malakhov, do you understand? "

" I understand, Comrade Commander," Sizov replied, laughing.

The man in the raglan coat had put spirit into all, and if he had not returned to the bridge, such jokes and questions would have gone on until morning.

" Who was that? " the men asked when he had left.

" Batya or, rather, Captain Nemo to you," answered a passing sailor.

" Who? " the men asked again.

" The ship's captain," the sailor answered, surprised that the men of Siberia and the Urals did not yet know their popular captain's nickname.

There were many anecdotes and tales about the captain in the raglan coat. He had a reputation for phenomenal bravery, for his profound hatred of women, for despising all writers and not caring much for political workers.

---

* The Malakhov Kurgan (*kurgan*=tumulus or barrow) is a plateau, the highest point in the vicinity of Sevastopol. Its storming and capture by the French in 1855 decided the fate of the town in the Crimean War.

Under pressure from friends he had married five years before " for decency's sake," but his family life was restricted. Whenever he reached port he sent a passenger to see his wife, taking her money, all kinds of documents, and a note, the text of which was almost invariably the same: " Cannot come ashore. Straightening up a scandal." In fact, as soon as his ship was tied up, the captain used to spend his time overhauling machines, inspecting gun turrets and other parts of the vessel, getting ready for the next journey.

Because of a favourite practice of his, all his officers knew some English, German, and Italian. " Today," he would say, " all orders will be given in Italian." At first everybody worked with dictionaries, but after a fortnight this was forbidden. Before the war this captain was well known along the Black Sea coast for his brilliant seaman-ship, his skill at bluffing, and the elusiveness of his destroyer, which he learned to navigate close to the Crimean cliffs.

The alert announced that a German reconnaissance plane was overhead. Old whiskered sailors and young lads in Spanish berets were at their guns. The infantry lay still. We knew that close behind the reconnaissance plane would come torpedo-carriers and bombers in force and that we should have little chance.

As soon as the plane left we changed our course and rapidly made for the German-held coast near Yalta. Then, turning, we traced a course close to the coast in the twilight until we reached Sevastopol. They were looking for us somewhere in the open sea while we care-fully picked our way through the mine fields in the approaches to the port. Darkness fell as we entered the harbour. We were at Sevastopol.

CHAPTER IV

WE drew near to our landing-point. The sun, which had been gradually sinking into the sea, disappeared as suddenly as if it had fallen on its back. But for some time the distant heavy storm clouds glowed with its light. Then night came on swiftly and persistently, and the darkness made the sea appear to grow deeper. As we approached Sevastopol, the waters were calmer, for the storm had long ago swept on to the land. The lights of the Chersonese Lighthouse began to flash—it was the only light that was not blacked-out in Sevastopol. As soon as it took up its task of showing us the way, the sides of the lighthouse were lit up by flashes of exploding bombs and shells.

The men who stood at their posts below this guiding light and among its lamps and lenses, opening up the path of life to our vessel, expected death at any moment, for they had learned respect for German marksmanship. But they kept their lights burning and the Chersonese beacon, as before, guided ships to Sevastopol—as before, but not the same as before. Every sailor in those waters, upon seeing that familiar welcome beam, knew that it did not beckon to happiness and rest, and that the glittering path it traced across the water was no way to a cosy hearth. Now the quivering light said: " Soon, soon you will cross the threshold of your destroyed homes. Soon you will see what the Germans have done to your capital. We are glad the enemy did not sink you in the open sea, for to die here on shore is to become immortal. Be patient, for soon you will be able to avenge."

It was not only to me that the Chersonese Lighthouse flashed that message, but to all who stood silently around

35

me, knowing that their hour of action was approaching. The infantrymen's spirits rose, on knowing that land was near. These men loved their land. They understood it and felt for it. That was why they had come to defend the heights of Sevastopol. They knew that their Ural and Siberian lands without the Caucasus and Crimea were too narrow for the Russian people and all who, with them, were building Socialism.

Our destroyer reduced its speed. It was passing along the narrow channel and threading its way in a series of complicated turns through the mine fields, where one false move would mean immediate disaster. At the beginning of the defence of Sevastopol the Germans allowed our transports and warships to move freely into the harbour. Then at the entrance of the bay they laid mines, closing the channel and trapping the ships in the bay, where they became easy targets for German bombers. The vessels which were lying at anchor endured the onslaught of dive-bombers and torpedo-carrying aircraft. Around them whole sections of mine fields were exploded, throwing gigantic fountains into the air, so that on the stillest days the ships were tossed like corks by the surge of the waters, in miniature storms as fierce as any that are weathered at sea. It seemed inevitable that the vessels would perish as the German bombs caused mine after mine to explode around them. One after another the sailors jumped from the ships, the young and the bewhiskered old tars, to swim not to the coast but to the mines. They pushed the floating mines before them, formed groups, and dragged them by loose cables to the shore. That is how a way from the bay was reopened, and ship by ship, with guns barking angrily, they slipped out of the trap. Many men perished in the mine fields. Many bodies were torn apart by exploding mines. These men died so that the ships could return with munitions to Sevastopol. They returned. Not a single one of them was sunk at the entrance to Sevastopol Bay.

At the place where, by the order of Admiral Kornilov, nine sailing ships of the Russian Fleet were scuttled during the Crimean War, a floating battery was established. It was sited on the blunt middle section of an unfinished warship which the Navy had towed from the Nikolayev shipyards during the evacuation and on which were mounted heavy long-range machine guns and anti-aircraft artillery. During the bitter winter cold and the spring storms this square steel fortress which was gripped by enormous anchors, poured fire at German bombers, E-boats, torpedo-carrying planes, and even at submarines which were trying to attack Sevastopol transports.

During one winter storm the floating battery dragged its anchors. Engineless and rudderless, it floated out to sea, where it was in danger of being smashed against the rocky coast of enemy-held territory. Realizing that the helpless battery was at their mercy, German coastal batteries opened a dense fire, and squadrons of bombers threw two hundred bombs at it. Shells racked its decks, and the streams of water which gushed into holes torn in its sides immediately froze. Two of the crew went mad. The rest, 120 strong, scorning the fact of their apparently hopeless position, scrambling and slipping over the frozen decks, though many of them were wounded, went on fighting. The floating battery was forced by the sea against the shore. They took their machine guns, tommy guns, and grenades and jumped into the icy water, and so violent was their assault that they gained a footing on land, where they held their lines all day till the abatement of the storm allowed our light craft to approach and tow the battered hulk back to its original position. During the entire period of the defence of Sevastopol not a man of this battery came ashore.

I was on the battery much later, when it was floated into another position, covering with its furious fire the Chersonese Lighthouse. One hundred and twenty steel-helmeted men, dressed in blue overalls, with their faces almost black from wind, sun, and the grime of the front, had clambered over the guns and were waiting for the attacks of the dive-bombers. The constant strain through which these men had lived had turned most of them grey. Showing me the guns, the captain said: " As usual we stand about to die." The Marines and pilots of Sevastopol had nicknamed the battery " Don't Touch Me," but those who knew what torture its crew lived through every day called it the " Club of the Seven Times Hanged." No other names were ever heard in Sevastopol for this old square hulk without bow or stern.

We had reached the harbour—Sevastopol at last. The unhappy city was enveloped in flame and smoke. The Fascist knife was at its very throat. High in the sky hundreds of beams from searchlights, Russian and German, crossed like sharp silver swords in an aerial duel. A plane caught in the traversing beams slipped and turned like a hunted hare blind with fright—vainly. Like a streaming torch belching sparks, it swept down through the smoke pall overhanging the darkened Korabelnaya Harbour and crashed with a long, loud explosion. Like banners dipping as a cortège passes, the searchlights slowly inclined towards where the plane fell. Somewhere along the coast, with small trembling flames, its debris burned itself out. Satisfied and for once in agreement, the beams climbed towards the sky again, suddenly to vanish or with sweeping tentacles to probe distant sectors.

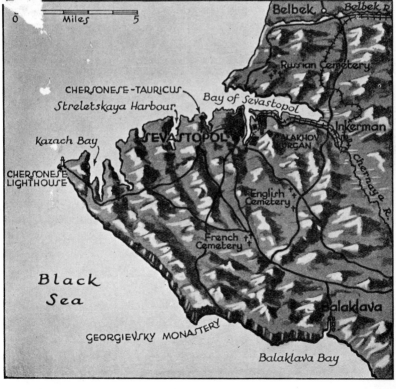

MAPS OF THE CRIMEA AND OF THE NEIGHBOURHOOD OF SEVASTOPOL

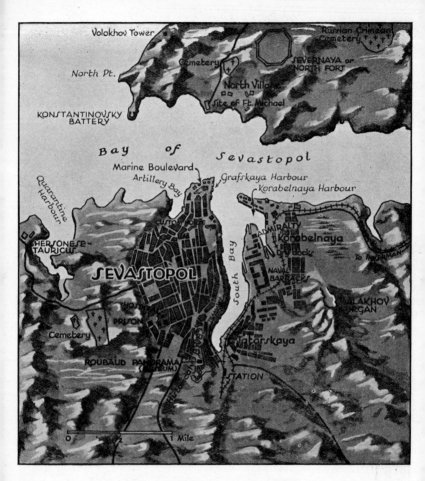

MAP OF SEVASTOPOL AND ITS DEFENCES

The sky above Sevastopol gleamed with thousands of explosions, trembled and rocked. Shells and high-explosive bombs burst, tracer bullets wove their deadly pattern, flares attached to parachutes burned brilliantly and lingeringly. The light of incendiaries, in the grip of which many of Sevastopol's houses were being consumed, threw such a glow over the city and harbour that one could read by it. The sea was still, and the surface of the bay mirrored the inferno that was raging along the shores. To the left of the mole where we landed, barracks, warehouses, and other harbour buildings were blazing. From time to time there was a terrifying crash. As I watched, the only remaining wall of a long-since demolished building slowly lurched into the sea.

"We are lucky. It is a quiet night," said Captain Nemo, and he meant it seriously.

"What is it like when it is not quiet?" I asked.

"Tomorrow in the day-time you will find out," the captain replied.

Our vessel was tied up. As soon as the gangways were thrown out, unloading began. The chaos ashore was indescribable. Hoarse voices raised in command, altercations, arguments, or oaths, wailing and brief sharp cries, screams of hysterical women that pierced one's heart. A hundred people jostled, shoved, and ran aimlessly hither and thither. They formed dense knots through which others, elbowing their way, broke only to stumble on the quayside, then got up to fight their way to their objective. Then, finally reaching it, they found it was not the place they wanted to reach. Bewildered children screamed for their parents. It seemed doubtful whether the quay would support the great and unwanted crowd with their luggage, sacks, and cases of incongruous household objects.

The Last Days

Five barges pulled up to the quay. On them lay wounded Marines and Red Army men in bandages. Many of them were groaning. Young women, almost girls, climbed the slippery, narrow gangways, straining under loads of wounded. One gangway broke and girls and wounded men fell into the water. Someone shouted ; another cursed the man who shouted. Sailors from the destroyer jumped into the water and helped the girls rescue the wounded. The barges discharged their melancholy cargo, and the wounded were laid on the baggage of evacuees with their hands taut, unbelieving, necks encased in plaster of Paris, heads or bodies bandaged. They lay on their backs waiting to be taken on board the destroyer.

Into this shoving, swirling crowd the infantrymen from the ship moved with vigour, pushing away from the gangways old men and women who were waiting to be evacuated, till they had formed a line and had answered their roll call. They were going straight to the front.

The crew, who rarely slept, so constant was the crowd of people and the mass of cases in their quarters, unloaded the cargo themselves, working the noisy derricks quickly but efficiently. Soon the quay was crowded with new aeroplane engines, boxes of shells, bombs, freshly painted machine guns, mobile artillery, flasks of oil and acids, spare parts for tank caterpillars, sacks of flour, salt, canned meat, and much more besides.

The pile grew between the ship and the waiting evacuees and wounded. I remember two voices among all this confusion, one a woman's crying: " Where is my aspidistra? " the other that of a tall gaunt Red Army man who was quietly passing through the crowd with a child's toy rifle in his hand, phlegmatically shouting:

" Whose rifle? Whose rifle? " As I listened, the voices were drowned by the clamour of people coming aboard the destroyer.

The crew had just finished unloading the munitions from deep holds and now began to take on the thousands of pieces of evacuees' luggage. No restriction had been put on what could be transported. Even plants were allowed. Only in this way could the stubborn reluctance of the people of Sevastopol to leave their beloved city be broken down. That is why now, on abandoning their homes, these people were taking with them every object which reminded them of their childhood, youth, or old age, of their joys and woes, anything that in unknown cities or villages could bring back to these southern people memories of their life beside the sea. The Navy understood this, and with solicitude sailors carried up the gangway ancient models of sailing ships, knick-knacks, family portraits framed in lifebelts, old seascapes, deck chairs, ornamental tables and screens which for decades had stood unmoved in front parlours.

The destroyer had little time to turn round. She had to leave one hour before dawn. The feat of unloading and reloading was carried out almost miraculously. Operations for which the barest minimum in peace-time had been twelve hours were carried out in one hundred minutes—a sign that all the noise and chaos which had made such a shocking impression at first was, in reality, only the deceptive façade of brilliant discipline and order.

The sky continued to flutter nervously with flashes of the battle. Next to the pier, on a steep bluff, yet another house had started to burn. Its roof fell in with a metallic scrunching sound. Momentarily flames ceased to burst from its windows or doors ; then with renewed violence tongues of fire met at the top of the brazier and leaped skywards in a single gigantic blaze.

In its light the nearby streets and alleys showed up. Dark empty houses, abandoned by their owners, looked forbidding and stern. Crowded on the decks of the destroyer, women, children, and old men, and their husbands, brothers, or sons seeing them off, turned their backs on the sea and looked long and silently at the burned, demolished homes. There were no cries, and if they wept, it was very quietly. And the tears were not those of desperation, cowardice, or even bewilderment, but tears of hatred, anger, or revenge. At this silent moment of farewell between men staying to defend Sevastopol and women leaving for the " Big Land " an unspoken oath was taken—to remember everything, to repay everything.

The blazing house on the hill was a new target for the German long-range artillery. Over our heads heavy shells screamed to shatter its high walls. Its red-hot girders, sheets of corrugated iron, piles of bricks, and burning furniture were avalanched on to the quay and were threatening the stacks of unloaded munitions. The enemy was directing his aim gradually lower. One more shot and all the work of the destroyer would be wasted. Everyone turned to the task of saving the cargo from fire. With heads, bodies, or wounded limbs badly burned, they nevertheless stuck to the job, determined to save such a prize from the spreading avalanche of flames. And they won and rescued, if not everything, at least that which was most urgently needed. The departure of the destroyer was delayed thirty dangerous minutes.

Amid these tears, the hurtling of shells, the skirmishes with the fire and the business of loading, the commissar of the destroyer was approached by a small, pale-faced man who took out a notebook and in his toneless voice asked: "How many meetings did you hold during the trip? Did you read any articles aloud?" The commissar looked coldly at this intruder and said abruptly: "We had a meeting to discuss the liquidation of fools like you. It was a very successful meeting, too. Aren't you ashamed to ask such questions when there isn't a man you can see here who has slept for the last ten days or eaten except at night on the journey back? Get away."

The little man fidgeted where he stood for a moment and then went away. I saw neither shame nor regret in his dim fish-like eyes. He was the only senseless bureaucrat I met in Sevastopol, fortunately. When this was over and the zealous party official had vanished, the commissar remarked: "Not even bullets seem to hit such creatures. To hell with him—the insensitive, tactless idiot!"

I had to watch the whole drama of the unloading of the ship from on board, for I had not been allowed to go ashore. I awaited the arrival of the Admiralty official with anxiety, for already, through his junior on board, he had refused me permission to land. His deputy had apologized for my trip being in vain and kindly offered me his cabin for the return journey, being apparently certain that any attempt I might make to stay in Sevastopol would fail.

Shortly before we were due to leave, a short stout man in a tightly buttoned overcoat approached me and said without introducing himself: "Show me your papers. I am going to mark on them that you arrived here and left again on my instructions. You realize that this is no place or time for literature. Don't you see what is going on here?"

"Yes," I answered decisively, and remembering my success with the Novorossiisk chief, I went on: "I certainly see and understand what is happening here and that is why I demand, not merely ask, to be put on shore." But though my words were firm, I had doubts within me. I was already tortured by the fire-racked city with its incessant roar beating on my nerves. What could day be like? But remembering Batum and his crew, and the infantrymen already on the way to the front, and seeing around me the distorted and disfigured wounded, I realized that to return would be a betrayal.

The situation obviously called for decisive action. I said to the commissar: " Very well, I will tell the editor of *Pravda* that you personally "—I stressed that word—" without the sanction of the Admiralty, prevented me from describing what is happening in Sevastopol."

The words " personally " and " without the sanction of the Admiralty " apparently made an impression on the commissar, and stepping aside, he ordered the guards to let me pass. I had agreed that as soon as the destroyer left I would accompany him to his headquarters.

The gangways were taken up, lines were freed, and I saw Captain Nemo in his black raglan coat giving curt orders on the bridge. Slowly the vessel drew away from the mole, and last messages and looks passed between her passengers and the men grouped on the quay. The destroyer turned sharply and headed for the Konstantinovsky Battery. A lucky journey was the wish of those who watched the ship off. Lucky in battle was the wish of those who saw Sevastopol receding.

When the ship was out of sight someone shouted: " Where is Petrov? " Everybody began searching for Petrov and then realized that during the turmoil of the departure Petrov had bolted and got on board the ship leaving Sevastopol. It was surprisingly unpleasant. Apparently nobody expected such cowardice from him.

For a moment his comrades hesitated. Then they grimly swore and spat in the direction of the ship and moved away. " So you were anxious to save your skin, you hound," someone shouted.

CHAPTER V

THE quay emptied quickly and I was left alone among the smouldering timber and cases of munitions. Nobody came to me and, being afraid to stay in this precarious situation, I wandered among the shells and bombs in search of the Admiralty official. I was challenged by a sentry almost at once. True to the Marine custom, he wore machine-gun belts crossed as bandoliers over his sturdy chest and had a knife in his belt. He carried a tommy gun. Having found out that I was from Moscow, he began tentatively to pump me: " How is it in Moscow? Has Moscow also had a few scratches? " and he led me to a dugout where the commissar was talking to lorry-drivers.

They had been shifting cases from the quay into underground shelters and to the front from the moment they landed. Conferring on routes, the commissar said: " You won't be able to reach this place. The bridge has been blown up. What? The main road? That is blocked too. And that road is no good either. It would take you a couple of days to pass those two craters." There was a short young Armenian of sturdy build who apparently had heard the order.

" Now," he said, " give me some ammonal and we will blow up the debris and get through the side roads and come out on Inkerman Highway."

" All right. Take it," the commissar replied, and went on to the quay, towards a cutter moored there.

At this moment a man appeared from the water, breathing heavily. He took off his dripping jacket. " Hell, I got back at last. I was saying good-bye to my wife and the damned ship left." It was Petrov, who had been cursed so roundly for wanting to save his skin.

I left with the commissar for the Admiralty in a cutter. We crossed from the northern to the southern harbour and ten minutes later went ashore at a wooden landing stage in front of a small, partly ruined house. The cliff rose immediately behind it, and on the cliff stood two large two-storey houses with holes in their fronts through which you could see the moonlit sky.

The tunnel which opened in the face of the cliff was ingeniously camouflaged with a projecting concrete barricade, behind which a naval patrol was on duty. We were let in at once and entered Naval headquarters— the nerve centre of Sevastopol's defence.

In the light the commissar was revealed as a smartly-dressed, pleasant-looking man. He led me now into the reception room of the commander-in-chief, a narrow room which was spotlessly clean and tidy. A small table crowded with telephones, bells, and switches, was surrounded by adjutants of the members of the Military Soviet. They were young men, impeccably dressed, clean-shaven, polite, and efficient. Their decisions were made quickly and succinctly.

The room was filled with high-ranking officers who were accustomed to report personally to the Military Soviet every night, coming in from the principal sectors of the defence system. From their appearance and expression, as well as the way in which they carried their guns or wore their uniforms, their manner of giving orders and explanations, you could tell how they would behave in front-line positions, airfields or the main defence works, at the numerous battery placements or in the trench dugouts which they had left temporarily to confer in this underground headquarters. Most of them were bandaged, but their faces showed no signs of distress as a result of their wounds. A little pallor was the only outward sign.

Every officer was accompanied by a political commissar, for in Sevastopol they were inseparable. Together they were decorated, together they died, together they were reprimanded, and together at that crucial moment when personal example proves decisive, they went into attack. In temperament and behaviour, in their way of issuing orders, and in appearance, the commanders and the commissars were in complete contrast. The commanders were quick, lively, persistent, and young. The commissars were calm, reflective, and some seemed passive, dull, even flabby. Three commanders made a strong impression on me. The first, a man of medium height with a nervous tic, was wearing the red braid of a full general's uniform—the only braid in the room. Everything in his appearance, especially the softness of his face with his glinting pince-nez, reminded me of a retired schoolmaster. There was nothing conventionally military about him except his uniform, yet this general was the gravest and the most combative of all those who were present.

A long time afterwards I was told that he was considered to be a vain man, who had surrounded himself with writers and journalists to get publicity. That was what angry tongues said. The fact is, I know that this general, in the way he approaches people, in the freedom of his speech with his men, and in his powerful influence over them, resembles the famous Marshal Suvorov.* In approaching Red Army men he would use an old-fashioned formal greeting: "How dost thou feel, Thy Friendship?" And while putting a man's untidy cap in order for him, he would start a long friendly conversation. This brave general still lives and fights.

Near him in headquarters, sharing a chair with the commissar, around whose shoulders his arm was flung, sat a young man with the blue air-force insignia, and, to my surprise, the silver stars of a general on his collar. Lean, dark-complexioned, with black hair, he looked more like an overgrown youth than a young man. As he talked, gaily and decisively, all listened to him attentively, obviously recognizing his authority. His left pocket was pierced with several neatly stitched holes for decorations. Whereas the others carried tommy guns, revolvers, or old-fashioned pistols in silver-monogrammed wooden holsters—relics of the Civil War—he was unarmed, but as he described an incident that happened that day on the airfield, he tossed and caught a hand grenade. Someone said: "That might explode." "It doesn't matter," the airman replied, laying the grenade aside. "You're the kind that won't be killed." Everybody laughed.

The young general, who was known as the "King of the Sevastopol Sky," had until recently been an active pilot and had been decorated by the Soviet Union for his extraordinary valour, which had become quite legendary. He was known to have survived a single combat with

---

* Alexander Vasilievich Suvorov (or Suvarov) (1729–1800), one of the greatest and most famous of Russian generals.

twenty-five enemy planes. His chief asset was that he combined personal recklessness with weighty experience and cool calculation. While he lived, many German air attacks met with failure.

He perished, quite unnecessarily, soon after I had seen him. While inspecting some aircraft repair shops with a visiting aviation chief, they drew near to a hangar. They were warned that an enemy dive-bomber was overhead. The young general looked up, saw the plane, and made up his mind to take cover, but noticing that his chief was paying no attention to it, he waved his hand and walked on. All who took cover were unharmed, but both generals were blown to pieces.

The third person who impressed me in that company wore a naval uniform. Leaning against the wall, he talked to no one and apparently was plunged in deep thought. He was a handsome man of the Russian type, with a full beard. Every few moments he glanced at a heavy gold watch, fixed to the bottom buttonhole of his jacket by a gold fob chain with an anchor. He frequently called the commissar over to him and made careful jottings in a notebook. It was clear that he was carefully preparing for a conference. He was one of the first to be summoned into the commander-in-chief's room. Stretching himself, straightening his jacket, and paying careful attention to the crease in his trousers, he walked smartly from the room.

To many it was a mystery how this man, who was a highly qualified artillery expert, could, after a day of violent battle, appear at headquarters so neat and well ordered in appearance. The mystery was proved very simple of solution. One day a shell burst near a car standing outside headquarters. The machine was damaged and overturned. In the morning a patrol found

49

scattered outside the Admiralty the clothes brushes, shoe polish, and coathanger on which the commander used to hang his jacket when on his way to a conference.

After they had seen the commander-in-chief, the commanders did not linger in the anteroom, but went straight back to their posts. After a while I was invited into the room of a member of the Military Soviet and was received by a short, stooping, but plump man with soft, gypsy-like eyes. He questioned me closely. How was Moscow? What was the " Big Land " saying about the Navy? How long was I staying? Did I like the sea? Had I been in Sevastopol before? He watched me closely, appraising me as I answered every question exhaustively. Then he tersely summed up the local situation, telling me that the German third offensive was in progress, and wished me good night till the next day.

I liked this man immensely. He belonged to the ranks of the military intelligentsia, whom you find mostly in high positions in the Red Fleet—modest, sociable, and well educated.

I was given permanent lodgings at the Admiralty, with the right to take my meals there. I was also given a suit of uniform too big for me which I thankfully exchanged for my civilian dress, which had become intolerable to wear in Sevastopol.

The tension and excitement of the atmosphere at the Admiralty defies description, but those who knew Petrograd in 1918 say that it reminded them of the Smolny* at the time of the October Revolution. Its narrow corridors, with arched ceilings, led deep into rock. Dim electric lamps, supplied by local storage batteries, helped

* Originally a convent, founded in the eighteenth century in St. Petersburg. It was taken over by the Petrograd Soviet in 1917 as headquarters of the Bolshevik Revolution. From there Lenin directed the uprising, and the organization of the Bolshevik Government.

one to grope one's way to the three tiers of steel-framed bunks which, covered with neat sailor blankets, lined the walls. In the gloom, people jostled or bumped into one another. Many doors opened off the corridors into small rooms where tense, energetic people worked, and from them you heard snatches of telephone conversations, radio voices, signals, and the rattle of typewriters, insistent voices of switchboard operators, the uproarious laughter of writers of anti-Fascist leaflets, the slow, studied words of the decipherers, the occasional screams of the wounded, the abrupt answers of officers on duty, and the clanking of a sentry's tread; the clear voices of men reporting from the front, the rattle of plates from a mess room, or the harsh snores of the sleeping.

The largest of these underground suites had its own telephone system, several radio stations, two Diesel engines, a drinking water and drainage system, a restaurant, a barber shop, and many other services deep in the rock. But in spite of its size it lacked air, although it had pumps and ventilators. When the municipal supply of electricity failed and one Diesel broke down and the fans stopped, the crowds of people working below the ground rapidly consumed the air and it became difficult to breathe. It was a tragic sight to see the women workers, who were unsparing in their toil. Their pale sallow eyes were inflamed day in and day out, they gasped for breath at telephones or typewriters, in canteens and in barber shops. Occasionally relieving one another at work, they took in their arms their children, who sweated in their sleep, and stood in the trenches outside, breathing deeply the sharp sea air. Here at the entrance to the cave it was customary for all who had a spare moment for a cigarette or fresh air to foregather.

But such relief was rare and it was often interrupted

51

by shrapnel or bomb splinters, which drove all underground once more, and then again they would hear the
ceaseless sounds of the "Underground" Navy. The
Navy switchboard operators were speaking: "Yes, yes,
switchboard." "Don't trouble Saturn." "Wait, Big
Bear." "Yes, I hear you, Navy." "Kutuzov is busy.
No, he is not sleeping. He is busy. Wait, he was asking
for you today." "Navy, Navy."

Bare to the waist, the radio operators were slipping
their headphones on and off and dictating urgent messages: "Forewaters Yalta"—each letter was spelled out
slowly—"Ship damaged. . . ." Another voice broke in,
cursing an interrupting German voice: "Fritz, Fritz, stop
your chatter. Fritz, get off the line. Well, I will jam you
too." From another room operational orders were being
dictated and repeated: "O-24 searchlight crew: Light
the entrance of the bay for incoming transport. Women
and children evacuees from a sunk transport are being
picked up by following warships. Anti-aircraft batteries:
Obey special instructions not to give away positions by
unnecessary gunfire. Ask Streletskaya Harbour to prepare for the landing of three hydroplanes with air reinforcements. Streletskaya expecting a submarine with
fuel. Forty minutes ago the Germans directed fire on the
harbour. Instruct the Thirty-fifth Battery to shell the
Germans."

In the room nearest to where I was trying to sleep sat
the officer on duty for the night. This tired, nervous man,
who was sitting at a small table, phlegmatically recorded
in the log everything that happened during his shift. His
was the record of death and catastrophe, the record of
Sevastopol's minute-to-minute life. Every trace of fear,
all aversion to wounds, all sorrow for the perished or
bewilderment before death had long since atrophied in

this man. It seemed clear from the way in which he monotonously questioned details or facts that he had become completely weary and indifferent to the war.

"Smirnov? Yes, I hear you. Shell hit what? Cutter? All lost? What does 'all' mean? I need figures. Were you there at the time? No? Find out definitely how many were killed and ring me back. Control? What's the matter? What? No leg? Where is it? Torn off? Oh, well, I will send a doctor right away."

The man he was talking to was the sentry at the entrance, whose leg had been blown off. I discovered later that this man was far from indifferent to the events he had to record methodically. He did his duty dispassionately, swiftly, and efficiently.

The voice continued calmly: "Quay. Yes, I hear you. Yes, what? All right, I will write it down. The evacuees who failed to take off in the transport were thrown by an exploding shell into oil . . . into the oil lake burning on the harbour surface. No hope of saving them. I am repeating the last sentence—no hope of saving them."

Then began the usual early morning bombardment, just before dawn. All voices were drowned by the fearful noise of bombs exploding on the rock above. So heavy were they that in places the rock was cleft and it seemed that at any minute these corridors, rooms, and dugouts would cave in to bury completely, below the rock, these tireless, toiling people. With every new crash overhead a naval officer who was sleeping in the same room counted aloud:

"Sixteen, seventeen, eighteen."

At first I thought he was dreaming, but he spoke so loudly that I grew impatient and called: "What are you counting for?"

He turned to me and said: "If they are landing in

the crater overhead, it only needs five or six direct hits to break through."

" Isn't it pretty unlikely there will be direct hits just on the same place? " I asked.

" Not in Sevastopol," he replied, and went on counting : " Nineteen, twenty " ; but when, according to his calculations, we should have been smothered, we both fell asleep.

CHAPTER VI

DURING four days of terrible raids I had not left the underground headquarters once and could not understand those who, despite categorical orders to the contrary, went out in full daylight to see the ruins of Sevastopol. Pale, stained, and scarred they rushed back into the shelter expressing by their looks what was happening outside the Admiralty walls. They were angry, and if they had met the Germans they would have cut their throats.

In the evening, while sitting round the mess-room table, opinions were exchanged. Departmental chiefs, commissars, people from the " Big Land " on special missions, newly-arrived captains, and many others were present. Once during a discussion about the relative damage that was done to Sevastopol in the Crimean War and in this, a Naval officer entered the room. " That is Nakhimov," whispered my neighbour.

" Nakhimov? " I echoed, for Nakhimov, whom I knew about, had perished eighty-seven years before, when

54

struck by a bullet on Malakhov Kurgan. I was shocked by the newcomer's resemblance to the famous admiral, whose portrait is so well known to Russians.

Captain Nakhimov was of middle height, slightly bent, with a pleasant, ruddy, open face, and large, gentle black eyes. I remembered his cap with its curved peak giving him a slightly old-fashioned, romantic appearance. His real name was Alexeyev, but everybody called him Nakhimov, not because of his resemblance, but because he idolized the hero of Sinope* and imitated him in every possible way. Like the admiral, he had not married, holding that a sailor had no right to a private life. All his money he lent to others or gambled on lotteries or gave away to friends in need, so that sometimes he was left without enough for his own dinner. His admiration for Admiral Nakhimov was more than superficial or trivial; the resemblance, even to short side whiskers on his sunburned cheeks, did not annoy or repel one as is usually the case when one encounters so blatant an imitation. When I heard him talk and learned something of his mind, I realized that his hero-worship was based on that profound love of the sea for which Admiral Nakhimov was renowned.

A few weeks later the captain was killed on that same Malakhov Kurgan where the admiral had perished. Struck in the stomach by a bullet, death was slow and agonizing. With his face to the ground, and bleeding from ears and mouth, he lay in a welter of blood and mud, trampled by passing horses until in mortal pain he was borne into a shelter. In his last delirious moments the brave man screamed the famous Nakhimov order: "Friends, if anyone tells you that I order you to retreat,

* The Russians under Admiral Nakhimov destroyed the Turkish fleet at Sinope in 1853, early in the Crimean War.

kill him as a traitor. If I come to you and repeat it, kill me. Sevastopol must be held."

Now the captain was listening attentively to an officer who had been into the city and was describing its destruction.

"There is no town left. The houses are all roofless; you see the sky through holes in them. The streets are nearly all blocked by avalanches of rubble. You hear nothing but bursting bombs and shells. It is Pompeii."

"Pompeii," the captain interjected. "No, that city was damaged less. I have been there and have seen its ruins and I must say I had quite different thoughts in my head when I saw those and ours. There was no glory in the destruction of Pompeii. It just had no choice between life or death when that volcano boiled over. Pompeii is only famous because centuries afterwards someone excavated it. Now here in Sevastopol, if you will permit me to say so, nothing was predestined. Whether it had gone on existing or was destroyed depended on the will of its people. I am sure that Sevastopol would have remained intact if we had behaved like the French at Paris. The last and the present annihilation of Sevastopol was and is utterly complete because of a stubbornness of its defenders that is not like anything else that has happened since the idea of attack and defence came into people's minds."

All were of one mind with the captain, who, after draining three glasses of tea and asking permission from the mess president to withdraw, left the room. I never saw him again, but shall remember him all my life.

It was in this mess room in the evenings that I made my first friends in Sevastopol. Despite the fact that they were all commanders on different sectors of the defences, all specialists in rather narrow fields, and all bearing the stamp of staff officers, they were witty and interesting to talk with. While I was summoning up courage to leave the underground headquarters and go out into the town, I became close friends with several of them. There was a short, bald-headed man with the sly face of a priest. He was in charge of preparing documents to present to the Military Soviet recommending people for decorations. At night I used to go into his room, where he drew up his formal lists. He spread before me hundreds of biographies. In his bulky yellow files was buried material for countless novels, stories, or scenarios, a veritable Thousand and One Sevastopol Nights. For instance, there was the story of how one sailor without help saved his ship. The side of a destroyer had been torn by a bomb, and water was pouring in. The sailor simply piled hundreds of cork life-jackets against a bulkhead till there was no more room left for water and its flow was stopped. It was so simple that nobody at first believed that this lance corporal had done anything smart.

Once as the registrar pored over his files he turned in despair to me and said: "What can I do? They are all heroes."

"Well, aren't you pleased about it?" I asked.

"Of course I am, but where am I to get the decorations from? Who would give them to me? If only the extraordinarily brave are decorated, then many really brave men will be offended. Naturally it would be easier if people consulted me before they did these heroic deeds. Then," he said with a laugh, "I could tell which quota is already filled. Sizov, for instance, has shot down enough planes to get ten decorations, but where can I get them?"

"Yes," I agreed, "you have a hard job. Haven't you any left at all?"

He opened a drawer in his desk, showing me the medals that were ready to be given out. In this shallow drawer lay the equivalent of thousands of dead Germans, scores of smashed tanks and planes.

Of the time I spent in the Admiralty commissar's company, I especially remember his discussions with divers. These experts in the mysteries of Sevastopol Harbour reported every day to the commissar about material recovered from the bottom of the bay. They dived every night, and below, among old wrecks and skeletons of the dead, they examined rents in the hulls of recently sunk ships and loaded their baskets with unexploded bombs and shells. These divers were convinced that the real history of Sevastopol lay under the sea. They knew so intimately the small harbours and creeks of the coast line that they used to assert that on shore little survived of Sevastopol's monumental history of tragedy and victory compared with what lay below. There, unrecorded by historians or guide books, Sevastopol's past lay around them. In the submarine forests, among the water plants in the deep narrow creeks, and within their scaly grottoes the past lay undisturbed from the moment it plunged into those still limpid waters.

Their heavy leaden boots clanked against the ribs of ancient Greek galleys, against the torn hull of the rebel cruiser *Ochakov*, which was sunk by shore batteries during the 1905 revolt. They wandered among the sunken marble monuments of Chersonese, the half-buried anchors of sunken sailing ships, guns of batteries lost in the Crimean War when the Russians crossed from ruined Sevastopol to the north shore of the bay, and the still unsteady shapes of recently sunk cargo vessels. And here tireless divers picked up everything with which the Germans could be routed.

The commissar was insatiable. He knew that before Sevastopol the Germans had massed fourteen divisions with a huge force of aircraft and that these were now being hurled at the city in their third offensive. Wiping sweat from his brow and drinking yet more water, he carefully thumbed sunk ships' papers and bills of lading, asking persistently: "Where are those six aeroplane engines? Why haven't I had those cases of dry bread? Where are the bandages, the cotton-wool, and drugs? What are you doing there on the bottom? Playing chess with the dead?"

"Just that," replied the chief diver, "and you had better come and take a hand down below; then you will be satisfied that it is impossible to get up those motors. They are covered with piles of dead horses and cavalrymen in the hold. Drugs—" he hesitated—"I can't go there."

"Why not?"

"I have been a diver for thirty years. During that time I have seen things that drove people who were working next to me mad, or else they would come up grey-haired, but to go into that cabin where, if I open the door, dead bodies of children rush towards me—No, I can't and I won't."

"Well," said the commissar, "that means you are letting living children die for the lack of food and bandages."

The discussions ended as always with the divers going straight back to their cutters and down below. And in the morning the aeroplane motors were taken to the airfield, the bread and bandages were drying in the sun on shore, and the salvaged shells and cartridges on the way to the enemy through Sevastopol's sky.

After such discussions the commissar used to leave his

shelter and go to a ruined house followed by his chauffeur. They would climb up a fire escape to the second floor, where in the middle of a large room stood a bathtub. The room had no roof and only two of its walls were left. Sweating heavily, the commissar undressed, got into the tub, and soaping himself well while splashing in the water, would shout to his chauffeur: " Kolya, how is the air today? "

" Everything is in order; carry on," the chauffeur invariably replied.

Bombs would burst near by. The commissar would get out of his bath, curse the Germans, and return to the Admiralty to issue new orders, to confer and decree.

The only civilian in the Admiralty was the waiter. Among blue, brown, and black tunics, sea coats, and jerseys, mostly old and shabby, he was a distinguished figure in his white jacket bearing the gold-crested buttons of the hotel he worked in before the war. This old man, who had lived all of his life in Sevastopol, was an old-type waiter with the manner of an ambassador. He now served in the room where the High Command dined. Everybody in Sevastopol knew him as a veteran of the city.

One evening towards the end of my first week—a week of constant bombardment—I talked to him about his pre-war life. While talking about palaces and sanatoriums, magnificent rest homes famous for their kitchens, seaside restaurants of the neighbourhood, about sea-bathing and noisy cars packed with tourists, the waiter got on to the subject of Hitler. With a strong southern accent, he said: " Listen, did you ever see an institute named after Professor Sechenov? It was an absolute sea of ultra-violet rays. People used to go there on crutches and two months later they would be dancing. I ask you, where is the Sechenovsky Institute? Gone. Destroyed and smashed to pieces. After that, what can I say about Hitler? Hooligan [he used the picturesque word *Bosyak*]. And the Naval Library? Thousands of books in leather covers. Children used to go there and get any book they wanted, and, mark you, without paying. Then there were those statues and vases in the entrance. Where is the Library? Gone, destroyed—blown up. What can I say about Hitler? Bandit, gangster. And the Panorama?* Listen, people in Washington and New York used to leave businesses worth millions of rubles and get on ships and come here to look at it. Did you ever see circular pictures before? And what a terrible price it cost just to set it up with real guns, sandbags, and uniforms! So I ask you where is the Panorama? Gone. So what can I say about Hitler? Scoundrel, swine. To tell the truth, I am not excited. I have already applied for German and Rumanian prisoners to rebuild my house after the war, and if our commander-in-chief has decided to beat hell out of Hitler, then the matter is settled and I am not worrying."

I grew very friendly with a captain who was chief of communications. He was well set-up and sunburned, with quick penetrating eyes and a courageous look. He always talked hoarsely, as if with a heavy cold. He impressed everybody by his energy and good humour. His appearance was a signal for the immediate disappearance of any official stiffness, for his anecdotes and self-assurance were irresistible. He would undertake the most dangerous task smilingly and upon returning describe it in a way that removed all element of danger from it.

* The Panorama, formerly one of the tourist sights of Sevastopol, contained a huge painting, by Roubaud of Munich, representing realistically the storming of Sevastopol by the British and French in June, 1855. See Chapter VIII of this book.

During the first days of the terrible Sevastopol raids he invented the proverb: "Don't bother to have a hundred friends, but make certain you have a hundred doors ready." While drinking in the evening in the mess room, he would raise his glass, wink slyly, and say: "Toll the bells." The toast caught on immediately, and next morning all were raising glasses of tea with the words: "Toll the bells."

The captain had a fund of original but useful ideas, many of which he passed on to counter-propaganda groups working at the front. His was a leaflet which, under the title *Genug*, was a montage of military obituary notices from the German press. The Rumanian leaflets which had been prepared he had scrapped immediately with the words: "No good at all. It is local trade-union committee style. It is without pathos or sentiment. You have got to write so that those Rumanians will be so tearful that they will drop their rifles and run back to their Bucharest restaurants. Start with something like this: 'Rumanians, where are your violins?' Just as Averchenko did. Don't you remember how, in his stories about the last war, he wrote: 'The Rumanians retreated in orchestral groups'?"

There was plenty of sound sense in his jokes. He told me I was very foolish not to write a continuation of Eugene Petrov's *Diamonds to Sit On*.

"How can I finish somebody else's novel?" I asked.

"Nonsense, don't be prejudiced. Petrov will come along and grab the idea himself."

"Well, he is Petrov," I said. (Petrov did visit Sevastopol a little later and was killed on his way back to Moscow.) "All the same, how would you continue *Diamonds to Sit On*? It seems to me it is finished."

"No, you are wrong. It is not finished. You ought

to go on with Ostap Bender's adventures in the evacuated towns. Why, I have already had many good laughs thinking about it." He got up and, looking at a chair, said: "Perhaps the diamonds are here."

For the next few days everybody was talking about Ostap Bender's twelfth chair.

This clown was a hero. He often had to carry out some of the most dangerous tasks of the High Command. He landed on enemy shores on dark stormy nights, fought to the last cartridge, and was the last to embark on the return trip. I was told that he was among the vanguard which broke through the German coastal defences into Kerch Harbour during that famous winter landing operation. Following him through gaps were destroyers, heavier warships, and transports with munitions and reinforcements. On other expeditions he participated in surprise attacks when torpedo boats broke into enemy harbours and sank German landing barges, rafts, or cutters ready to attack our coasts. From such trips he would return coated with ice but cheerful. Devoted to his men, proud of their bearing and efficiency, he used to say: "You know what kind of men mine are. They follow me like poodles. Why? Because they know I am a beast who can kill and kiss and praise a brave man." A favourite song which he used to sing only in critical moments began with the words: "Open wide the gates, my darling."

He was singing it now as he read an old letter from his wife. "Listen, my friend, how she writes. Women ought to have style. You know it is very important. Some are good at loving and bad at writing. Some can't make love at all, but write admirably, and there are some who are no good at either. They are the ones we fall in love with just because they provoke us by their indiffer-

63

ence. But in all of that, by the way, we find traces of a capitalistic conscience."

Raising a glass of vodka, he downed it with " Toll the bells," which meant that a few moments later he and his commissar would be leaving to meet incoming ships at the port. After reading a few more favourite phrases from his wife's letters, kissing them, and putting them away carefully in a deep pocket, he took the commissar's arm and left the room with the words: " Follow me, commissar, the flags are out," and disappeared into the darkness.

At night the landing stages were illuminated with parachute flares and searchlights, and as soon as the German gunners got their range the shelling began. The scene was indescribable as the glowing stream of fire poured out upon the narrow target; the sound was unbearable as the dying screamed. Oil tanks, where submarines unloaded fuel supplies, blazed while cases of ammunitions on the quay exploded. Lorry-drivers rushed overloaded machines through the flame and smoke while the firefighters strove for mastery.

Here in this inferno, where many hesitated, the commissar and the chief of communications were in their element. Any thoughts of death, which both obviously harboured before leaving the Admiralty, were forgotten. They hurried from submarine to ship, from transports to hydroplanes, from lorries to depots, knowing that every moment gained lessened the chance of an explosion.

The main object was to maintain the tremendous tempo of loading and unloading. Faster, faster, faster. At dawn every vessel must be far away from the quay and clear of everything not too shattered to be useful. And every morning the front received its reinforcements. Never did these two men let the front down. But the price was very high and the methods used had to be ruthless. There were tense moments when this good-humoured fellow resorted to arms. Among the dock labourers were a number of convicts. One of them, apparently only too anxious for a German victory, had organized a group of malcontents and the work was going slowly. The chief came up to the convict and said: " Open your mouth and say ' Ah ' ! " The man did not move. The chief repeated the order and then shot him in the teeth, spattering those around with blood and brains. Then turning to the others, he said: " I want speed."

" This is for you," he said to another convict, who was showing great energy and speed on the gangways, and he gave him a thousand rubles. The effect was spectacular. The hold was empty in half an hour.

It was the duty of the chief and the commissar to see ships away from the mouth of Sevastopol Bay, and only when its boom was down again and the countless nets were in place did these weary men return to the Admiralty.

In such hours of prodigious toil it was the chief's high spirits that kept him and the others going. One night when a convoy was leaving the harbour, one of the ships, which was commanded by an old friend of the chief, reduced its speed, and the chief in a cutter that was following could hear a voice bellowing from the bridge: " Tolya—mines to port, mines to starboard, mines all around, screws caught in chains, and there is a sub-marine five yards away, dive-bomber right overhead—the crew is panicked. What shall I do? "

The chief's voice replied from the cutter: " Zhura, what the hell, are you crazy? "

Then the captain's voice came back, gay and optimistic: " All right, Tolya, don't get excited. Only a joke. Good-bye. No more fooling." The voice died away and the ship vanished out to sea.

When the main forces had left, Tolya stayed with the few to defend Sevastopol to the last. That was his duty as transport chief. To be ordered to leave last meant, of course, not to leave at all. Several days after the abandonment of the city this hero was seen among the wharves and quays getting the last cutters away.

For the first time he appeared sad. He embraced the commissar who was leaving for the " Big Land." " Toll the bells," he said in a low voice. And as the boats pulled out from the shore, he was seen standing alone looking long after them. No one knows what he did then, but I and the others who knew this gay ruthless hero and, heartened by his example, went to the " Big Land " to fight on in the spirit of Sevastopol believe that he made his way to the rocks singing: " Open wide the gates, my darling," with determination to sell his life at a very dear price.

CHAPTER VII

EARLY one morning when I was working on my notes in my room in the Admiralty, a man came in whom I had never seen before. He had the short, closely shaved head of a simple Russian and the face of a very tired man. He carried a water flask.

" Always writing? " he said to me. " All right, I will

sleep," and slipping the flask under his tunic, he lay, without undressing, on a bunk.

"Very well, if you want to sleep I will go away," I said, and picking up my papers, I went out. To my surprise, at the door was posted a fully armed naval guard.

Later in the morning I met the waiter and asked who was sleeping in my room. He glanced nervously around and then whispered: "The Admiral. He has got a squeamish stomach. It is no joke to have to run this business." Yes, the visitor was the commander-in-chief of Sevastopol's defence.

Feeling that I was already experienced by what I had heard and seen in the Admiralty, I plucked up enough courage to leave, and early one morning I went into the city.

Was it dawn—that very faint glow in the sky—or flashes of maddened guns? Slowly the ruins of Sevastopol emerged through the smoke screens and the lifting darkness. Another day of battle and explosion was breaking. The sky seemed to grow red-hot; then windows of blue opened. An angry frightened bird chased a restless wave, seeking fish. But the fish, stunned and deafened, had left the bay for the open sea.

As soon as the sun had reached the ceiling height of bombers and glinted on the distant artillery positions in the hills, dawn faded in the cloudy twilight of the battle's smoke.

For ten days Sevastopol's fires had been blazing, and a sea of flame now enveloped the city and the Korabelnaya district. I felt my nerves quailing before this frightful, gigantic panorama of the burning city which unrolled before my eyes. Half-submerged ships showing stern or bow projecting from the water still held trapped cargoes of unfortunate fugitives. The bay was the graveyard of these torn and shattered vessels. A fully-loaded schooner lay on her side with her masts sprawled on the surface, stretching towards the shore like the arms of a helpless drowning man. A large ship had turned over, showing her keel covered with seaweed and barnacles. There was one distorted humped stern, in the jagged shell-holes of which seagulls had taken refuge. They would emerge, to circle round the hulk and then plunge again into its deep wound. Cutters, barges, small ships, and floating derricks showed their funnels and masts above the water. A tanker was sliced in two. You could see her gangways and cabins open to the waves. In this scene of ruin the spectacle of Sevastopol Bay had a peculiar desolate appearance.

In lifeboats, among the corpses of men and animals in the blood-stained passages of the hulks, which were littered with glass and rubbish, the inhabitants of the houses nearest to the sea used to take refuge during air raids. They believed naïvely that bombs do not fall in the same place twice. They were wrong, for the Germans bombed the wrecks.

This was the seventh day of the air bombardment of Sevastopol. The Luftwaffe had divided the city into sections for the purpose of bombing, and systematically reduced each in turn, smashing block after block. Attached to the wings of the bombers were screaming sirens, the howls of which during a plane swoop were heart-rending. As these dive-bombers came lower you could hear their shrieks join and then drown Sevastopol's own sirens.

During the sixteenth hour of a raid in which some six thousand high-explosive bombs were dropped, I was watching how the bombers, the black cross markings of which I could see, were destroying the few houses remaining intact in one quarter of the town. The wonderful buildings of Sevastopol were crumbling before my eyes, and as each cloud of dusty smoke was rolled away by a bomb blast it opened a new perspective of the ruins. The earth and the sky seemed to be locked in some terrible distorted struggle in this narrow space.

There was no place in the town where instruments of death had not prevailed. No place was safe from bombs, land mines, or shell-fire from the enemy's siege guns. The sky was riddled like a sieve. The Theatre Square, Marine Boulevard, and Grafskaya Harbour were littered with fragments of shells and bombs. But that was not all. Pieces of rail, tractor motors, cart wheels, and ploughs were showered on the city in an attempt to shatter the nerves of its inhabitants and drive them to despair. Sevastopol was being bombarded with scrap metal. In their frenzy of elation at the superiority they had gained over the defences, enemy squadrons sought out women and children who were sheltering among the rocks while awaiting their turn to be evacuated. Powerful explosives cleft the ground and buried them in the debris beside the sea. Everything that moved—cutters, cars, and motor-cycles—was pursued and attacked.

This unprecedented expense of metal was due to the enemy's desire to reach a quick decision and subdue the city's resistance. The air offensive was in its eighth day, but the third land offensive had not yet begun. On our defence lines the Germans made 30,000 sorties and threw 50,000 bombs in all, and most of the activity was during the early days. The scenes of the destruction defy description.

Here is where a hundred thousand of the defenders of

Sevastopol in the Crimean War lie buried. Count Todleben, who built the famous bastions of that time, named it " Fraternal Grave." Now, beside men of the Black Sea platoons, of the Naval Garrison, Kamchatka soldiery, of the Vladimir and other regiments, in the rock and earth there lay snipers, anti-aircraft gunners, men of the coastal batteries, and pilots of Stormaviks. The dead were covered with a thin layer of earth. There was no time for burial. On a hillock, where a damaged plane lay, I read these words written in Church Slavonic script on a piece of a propeller: " Make room, you in the graves. Shift, you old sweats. A newcomer has joined you to prove his love of battle. Take him into your graves. He is worthy." They were written by the local sexton and bell-ringer of the Christian Chapel.

In search of the local oil reservoirs, the Germans completely desolated the cemetery. They bombed its ancient family chapels, marble monuments, and gravestones. The remains of the Crimean War dead were scattered, and fresh blood drenched their ashes. In the waters fringing the sea, coffin lids bumped against the shore among lumps of ice which were rapidly melting amid the debris of the town refrigerator, which had just been hit by a bomb.

About the ruined graveyard wandered a man who was naked to his waist, wearing an empty bandolier and a revolver holster. In his hands he held an abacus and clicked its balls in some obscure macabre calculation, chuckling all the while. This mad sexton had frightened many until some Red Army men tied him up and sent him away to the " Big Land."

Behind the cemetery lay a region which had been so badly bombed that it was impossible to determine where streets or houses had been. Here were craters that contained blood-stained water in which floated hands, limbs, legs, and torsos of children. Beside one such crater a poplar was blazing, while a miserable cat was screaming and clambering on its trunk. When the flames licked it the cat fell into the bloody mire, scrambled out, and ran into the sea.

Back from their familiar sorties, the pilots sent their photographs to be developed in secret laboratories. They were pasted together and shown proudly to the Command. They proved conclusively that Sevastopol had ceased to exist. German generals who studied the panorama of the abolished city were satisfied and issued medals. Now it seemed certain that Sevastopol would yield with a little shove. Troops were told they would be bathing in the bay in two days' time, and after that they would be given a long leave. Leaflets were showered on the city: _Wie Geht Es?—How Are You?_

Yet the town survived. Boiling with energy and hatred, it gnawed at the earth with bleeding gums. I was conscious of its fierce constrained breathing. Deprived of its existence above ground, with its building shattered, Sevastopol continued its struggling existence underground in cellars, abandoned quarries, or dugouts and toiled to be ready for the final encounter with the enemy.

One hundred and fifty thousand German bombs killed only 173 citizens. The nerves of the survivors remained steady. Sevastopol was not Cologne. All knew that the real ordeal lay ahead. Every morning they expected poison gas and every evening an enemy landing. They waited and they were armed. Their leaders hid nothing. That was why the people of Sevastopol had already held out for eight months. Though tortured by the bombing, they held their heads high.

Civilian Sevastopol walked with grenades, rifles, or tommy guns in its hands. These people loved the arms they knew how to handle. With machine-gun belts strapped around them and with knives and revolvers at their waists while they stood at factory benches or worked in offices, they were constantly vigilant to defend their homes and places of work. That those places were to be the last strongholds, all knew. Young men, old men, women, youngsters, the sick, everybody, joined the "Fighting Hundreds"—volunteer detachments of armed citizens.

I remember how one woman, old-fashioned in appearance and obviously of pre-Revolution origin, used to take timid steps for fear that the grenades which hung around her waist would explode.

It was now, for the fourth time, the "last day" of the Sevastopol battle—according to the Germans. But no white flag of capitulation was hoisted. Nobody even thought of that way out. Everybody believed in and worked for victory. They said that times had been worse, that eight months before, when the enemy suddenly broke through the Perekop Isthmus, which is the gateway to the Crimea, the danger was greater, for then the town lay open.

Then, instead of surrendering Sevastopol, boys from the training vessels were sent into the battle. They were called Marines. Comsomols, girls, teachers, and typists joined their ranks. The teachers and typists sang out of tune, sang the old Revolutionary songs, and, what was worse, they marched. They had no tommy guns, only rifles, and they did not know how to shoot. For officers, they had shopkeepers, clerks, and telegraph operators. The boys, clerks, Comsomol girls, and anti-aircraft gunners stopped the Germans. That was what had been.

72

It was a miracle that will be remembered in history. Now Sevastopol trained, well armed, and angry awaited the enemy.

Strange how on those days, the scent of flowers was sometimes more powerful than the smell of burning. Days passed. Three daily papers, the *Commune Lighthouse*, the *Red Black Sea Fleet Man*, and *For Motherland*, appeared with punctual regularity. In them you read: " Your heart will fill with hatred when you see this destruction. For every house, every brick, the Germans will pay with black blood. We will not forgive nor forget. . . . Danger hangs over the city. The third offensive has opened. We must be braver and more self-sacrificing. . . . The enemy is trying to sow panic among us with provocative information—trying to break our belief in victory. All who help him must be exposed and destroyed. . . . The town bristles with bayonets. We are ready to meet the Germans in the Sevastopol way— the Black Sea way."

The newspapers issued appeals: " Let every one of us be a hero in Sevastopol's defence. Let our descendants remember us with the same love and admiration that we have for the legendary participants for the first defence." Pamphlets were published as well as the satirical magazine *Rynda*. Newspapers, magazines, letters, and telegrams were delivered by a mobile post office. Whenever there was a lull, puffing, panting postmen would rush into the shelters. They were elderly men who knew the town inside and out, as they would sometimes laughingly say. Hour after hour they would make their way through the strange labyrinth of dugouts and shelters. Postmen dislike a town without numbers, and to satisfy themselves these men collected numbers off the damaged houses and methodically put them up on hundreds of cellars, caves, and shelters. As they came underground they reminded the fugitives from air raids of their former homes. They would come calling names of non-existent alleys, the numbers of vanished houses, thus soothing and at the same time irritating recent wounds. Undelivered letters were marked: " To be looked for after the war."

The postmen were as successful as field marshals. People would gossip with them, about the " Big Land " or about what was going on in the next cave. " Where is Antonina Vladimirovna? . . . Is it true that an underground cinema is open? . . . They say that under house No. 4 gold was found; that a merchant hid it there hundreds of years ago. . . . Is it true that Nicolai, who was so frightened of his wife, became the hero of Balaklava? " They used to ply the poor old men with jokes. " You had better tell your chief that when the town is rebuilt we want the post office to stay underground. You have never worked so well."

An old Jew who delivered newspapers was known as " Last Odessaite." He had reached Sevastopol on the last cutter, the *Dorothea*. The old man was being left behind and from the coast shouted: " *Dorothea*, come back—*Dorothea*." And *Dorothea* went back for him. His name was Rabinovich-Lyleyev. A long time ago he had been imprisoned for some now long-forgotten offence and was for a while in Tobol Prison, where, previously, a famous Decembrist had been exiled. When Rabinovich was liberated, he added Lyleyev to his name, thinking that this hint of the Revolutionary past would make his life easier. Also, he was fond of double names believing that they gave a man solidity and importance.

We had a talk. " Yesterday," he told me, " I appealed for the second time to be taken in as a member of the party. I am sure they will not accept me, but I will tell you why I decided to do it. In Odessa in the old days we didn't like power—any power, bad or good. We could not stand discipline even when it didn't mean shooting. Besides, we didn't understand how these young fellows who hadn't a penny in their pockets were building the Dnieper Dam and new theatres everywhere. Our thieves were dying of nerve strain. After the Revolution their clients' pockets were empty, for all the money was being spent on Socialism. They dreamed all night about the freedom of Odessa. Did we like the Soviet power? We didn't understand it, but respected it, most of all because it educated our children.

"That was no easy matter. What children they were! When I say 'our' I mean my own and those of my neighbour, who was the wife of a former municipal official, Madame Zeltz. On the last day of the evacuation Madame Zeltz shouted to the house manager, who wanted her to pay what she owed on her apartment: 'You'll please win the war for me first, so I'll know whom to pay and for what.' I heard this, and approached Madame Zeltz. I told her in the cold voice of a political worker: 'Madame Zeltz, you are a fifth-columnist.' Madame Zeltz didn't understand. I continued: 'We have lived with you all our lives on the same floor and I have fooled you all the time. I am really a member of the Communist Party and we are coming back to Odessa.' Madame Zeltz fainted and hit her head against her white-painted piano.

"On the ship I appealed for membership in the party. Before that I had exposed a former stockbroker who had been speculating in lifebelts. I was refused but I was not offended. A man who comes to be a Revolutionary through Madame Zeltz is not really worthy of much.

But today I read a postcard, and after that I asked again. Let them refuse me again, but I tell you when a man of my age cries, something is torn inside him." And he handed me an open letter. It ran:

Dear Unknown Friend:

This letter I am writing to you from Sevastopol. My letter is as stern as the town. My words are as heavy as the Navy. Dear unknown friend, this letter brings you woe, but I am fulfilling the last wish of your friend Gennady Godina. Your friend has perished. A cursed bullet ended his short, beautiful life. He died like a hero. His name is the symbol of Victory that thousands of Marines are taking into battle with them. He is buried in a wood under an old spreading oak. A friend of Gennady wrote down for you his last words, and an enemy shell ended his young life, too. Among the blood and dust I found this small blood-stained piece of paper and read the few words which were written by the hand of the dying soldier. Unknown friend, I don't know where you are now, but wherever you are, avenge his death. I know you will, for Russian women know they must.

Many of us grieve and many of us have our sorrows. This sorrow makes us ten times stronger and summons us to ruthless revenge. Revenge. The blood of Gennady calls you. Revenge bravely and fearlessly. If you should ever come to Sevastopol I will show you his grave and tell you of the Fascists' bestialities. Yesterday I saw an eight-year-old boy with both legs torn off by a shell. He was carried away on a stretcher. His mother, who was crazy with grief, was wandering among the ruins looking for the legs. But our heroes have no fear. Quiet and stern are the faces of the people of besieged Sevastopol. Dear unknown friend, every foot of our ground is stained with the hot blood and the bitter tears of children, mothers, and old people. You must avenge, ruthlessly, with your last breath.

Sevastopol Front.   *Vera Tomlina*

The old man was crying. He understood life. He put the letters and telegrams in a satchel and went quickly from the shelter, this man so strangely fated.

The next moment I heard shouts. I rushed out. "Who ever would have thought that I would die like Lensky," the old man said as he lay helpless on the ground. Even when wounded, the old fellow could not help joking. His wound was only slight, and after it had been bandaged he hobbled away. I thought him a hero.

On the cutter which took me to the North Side someone told me a story about two shopgirls. They came out of a house and were on their way to the biggest underground store on Matushenko Hill, in the quarry and in the tunnel of the northern hydro-electric station. The girls decided to go there by different routes, calculating this way—that if one was killed the other would probably get there to be on duty in time. The one who made the suggestion was killed. Although the other one was wounded, she got there. She does her work but doesn't want to go home again. I saw her, a child. Instead of buying bread with her ration cards, she takes sweets. She likes sweets.

I went to Inkerman Quarry by cutter. I had to get a permit from the military censor before I could send messages to Moscow. The place where the censor worked was under constant shell-fire. It was the most dangerous as well as the most inconvenient censor's office I had ever dealt with. A shell burst at its entrance every three minutes. Between whiles people went in and out of the tunnel in the rock. Those who did not wait for the interval never got anywhere at all.

At its entrance stood a small wooden booth where passes were issued. Judging by the phlegmatically slow manner in which he worked, the sentry must have imagined that he sat behind armour plate instead of flimsy walls. He had good nerves. My pass was faulty and an investigation was necessary. That took twenty minutes, during which seven shells burst.

At last, through a long dark tunnel, I reached typical Sevastopol, underground. The noise was incredible. The Admiralty was a monastery compared with this. The vast cellar was subdivided by heavy metal screens where hundreds of lathes hummed and rattled, turning out grenades. A tractor motor was roaring. It was generating electricity, but was puffing and smoking like a bad old samovar. When the motor stopped, the lights went out; immediately every worker lit a cigarette, and the cave glowed with hundreds of faint lights. It had been agreed among them that only when work was held up by a failure of current should there be smoking. On the same table a cook and a compositor worked side by side, the one peeling potatoes, the other setting up the front page of a newspaper. The potatoes lay among the type.

On bunks which were built in three tiers along the walls of the tunnels, the workers of other shifts slept. The strongest slept on top, where breathing was difficult. Below were the pale sallow children. Sometimes the children would play war games. The girls would wrap grenades in pieces of bright-coloured cloth to make dolls of them.

It was hard to sleep on those beds, for they were crowded with objects. There was no other place for luggage, for every corner was piled with the products of the machines. Messengers, department chiefs, journalists, and news-reel operators would hurry through the lines of benches. They and many others lived and worked here.

Poets were reciting their verses while painters were finishing sketches they had made at the front or were designing posters to stimulate the workers in a Socialist competition. A menu was posted on the wall. This was a formality, for everybody knew what there was to eat. A tired typist powdered her nose indifferently. The cashier paid out wages. The party secretary was preparing notes for reports on the situation. Someone was telling a tedious story about how and why he had not been killed. Kneeling at a small table, an engineer was shaving. A resting telephone switchboard-girl was playing a guitar.

The machines worked twenty-four hours daily, their noise not stopping a moment. With the tobacco smoke mingled the smells of the kitchen, gas, and stale air.

The whole front was relying on this factory for its grenades. It had been working for a long time, both here and above ground, where, to save hands during raids, the workers were sheltered under their machines. Some of the workers down here had burned hands as the result of putting out a fire. There were no invalids. Everybody was working. Before me was an elderly woman turning the handle of a stamping machine. She had no right hand. It had been torn away by a bomb blast. After leaving the hospital she had refused to go from Sevastopol to her native town. She was the best stakhanovite of the works and all were proud of her. Beside her was a beautiful young woman with a nursing baby at her breast, working a drill at the same time. She was not ashamed of her bare breast, and the men did not look at her. Every few moments the rhythm of the machine broke.

She readjusted it with her right hand while holding the tiny child to her breast with the other. Her son, who was called Ilja, never cried and everybody liked him for that. At night his mother took him into the fresh air for a while. He got excited and cried. " Never mind, darling," his mother soothed him. " Lie still. They will come and fly away again "—talking of bombers as if they were birds. Sometimes she charmed everyone by singing a lullaby. Among the machines, beds, and tables there wandered day and night a setter which was bored and was longing to be out hunting. Its master, the fore-man, sometimes took its head on his knees, rubbed it a little, and calmed it.

I went to the censor with one of my articles. The young man read it while eating noodle soup. Without comment, he stamped it—passed. I then had to go by water to the telegraph office, which was located in the southern part of the city. I managed to get out of the cave safely. The booth had been wrecked. On the way there our boat stopped near an unpleasant spot called Kilen-Balka-Step Valley—because it once had been a landing place for ships. Here German shells and bombs exploded constantly, searching for the supplies that had been unloaded during the night. The munitions were elsewhere, but that was no immediate consolation to us. Near the shore four shells burst fifty yards away. We expressed our feelings heatedly to the pilot: " How can you start on such a trip if you are short of petrol? " His only reply was a calmly delivered lecture about per-sonal bravery and the need for economy in fuel. In the coolest way in the world he told us that naturally he had spare petrol in the stern of the cutter, for he was not fool enough to go out short, but that now there was a war on and fuel had to be saved. That was why he had stopped here to wait for some passing ship to give him a tow for the last stretch. We pointed out that no other ship was in sight and begged him to abandon his economy campaign. Afterwards we all agreed he was a great man, but decided never to sail with him again.

I was now at the southern port. Shell-fire had reduced its bricks to powder. Even on quite short journeys you had to get out of a car twenty times to hide in trenches, lying there, perhaps, for as long as three or four hours. There was no alternative. If one wanted to get a job done, one just had to lie still, keep quiet and stick to it. And it was so important that everything should be done.

A shell burst near a lorry loaded with flour. A white mushroom grew in the air. The chauffeur survived "It doesn't matter; we will gather it up," he said, and he began to scoop up the scattered flour. The others preferred to take cover behind the intact sacks. The shelling continued unabatedly.

During such bombardments, when the offensive was at its height, no one was to be seen in town, not even soldiers. Despatch-riders took shelter, not because they were afraid, but because the order was to get through with the messages and return alive.

It was therefore particularly surprising, and created an atmosphere of unreality, to see a young, modestly dressed woman picking her way through ruins, carrying a bunch of fresh flowers. Not stooping as she walked down bombarded streets or passed gigantic craters, she walked with remarkable self-possession and precision. Afterwards I learned that every day she passed through ruined Sevastopol carrying a flaming banner of flowers to the cemetery where her husband, a man honoured among the defenders, lay buried. She rejected all advice to join the evacuees replying: "I shall stay here where my husband lies." And those whose advice and orders she thus rejected were, in the depths of their hearts, proud of her decision to stay in Sevastopol. As men they were proud that beside them, the fighters, sharing their dangers, stood this silent, modest Russian woman whose love was so bright and honourable. She became for them a symbol of the devotion and truth of all wives, the comradeship of all sisters, the measureless love of all mothers.

Every morning from ruined nursery gardens, under shot and shell, she gathered flowers and brought them to her husband's grave.

One morning she met Marines burying a comrade in the courtyard of a small ruined house. The sailors stood with bared heads beside a grave. She came to them, divided her bouquet, and placed flowers on the breast of the dead sailor. Among the ruins of a house by some chance a piano stood intact. She went to it and began to play Chopin's Funeral March. The Marines took their muskets and held them at present arms, motionless till the last sad strains had died away. Then one of the men approached her and said: " It is good to find that even here, among us, there are some intelligentsia. Thanks to you, we buried Kolya the right way, with musical honours. We shall take you to your grave, for our post is near by."

" Let us go together, comrades," the woman replied simply and quietly, and together they went.

CHAPTER VIII

DURING these days there sat in one of the cells of Sevastopol Prison a Nazi pilot. Bare to the waist, wearing nothing but tennis shorts and white summer shoes, he resisted the examining officer with surprising stubbornness. The officer would have liked to kill him, but he was a lawyer and had to restrain himself—though he did so only with difficulty, it was evident. The German's replies had been sharp and meaningless. Then, suddenly, all his haughtiness vanished. When the examining officer asked who the pilot thought would win the war, he replied: " Who will win the war? I cannot tell, I am no prophet. But that my generation has been completely annihilated by this war I do know, and nowhere more so than here at Sevastopol. That is enough for me and Germany to know."

The examining officer could not imagine what had happened, and when the prisoner offered to write a leaflet addressed to German pilots who were bombing Sevastopol he was dumbfounded.

But next day everything became clear. " Göring's Eagle " could not face the bombs that his colleagues were still raining on Sevastopol, many of which were falling near the prison. Already several cells had been wrecked and the foundations trembled dangerously below the remaining buildings. The German pilot became hysterical. A hundred times daily he shouted in broken Russian: " Evacuate me." His Ukrainian warder could not reply, but the head gaoler, who spoke German well, used to tell him: " Herr Oberleutnant, all I can guarantee you is a direct hit, sooner or later."

In the harbour, near the monument to perished vessels,

a passenger ship was sinking. The wind had carried away the smoke screen under the cover of which she had entered the bay, and she became a target for enemy planes as she zigzagged from coast to coast, followed by lifeboats. For a while the ship dodged eleven bombers skilfully. Three which were shot down crashed on their backs into the sea. By fighting their way through eighteen Heinkels, four Soviet planes scattered the bombers. Four to eighteen was typical Sevastopol odds. The fighters might as well not have been there, so far as saving the ship was concerned. Three bombs hit her plumb. Around the big steamship more than a thousand people struggled in the sea—Marine reinforcements. One of our fighters was hit. It turned over and over and crashed on the rocks. Its pilot had baled out, but he left a trail of smoke as he fell. The man was alight. The Germans were shooting at his parachute, ripping its fine silk. The burning man fell faster, going down now head-first; and managing to bring his arms forward, he plunged cleanly into the water.

When he reached shore all he said was: " Good fellow, Fritz. He put out the fire just in time: If he had not punctured my parachute I should have been roasted alive." He disentangled himself from the wet remnants of his parachute cordage, took out his watch, listened to it carefully, nodded when he found it still work-ing, and made his way to his airfield, where, after " apologizing " for his crash, he applied for a new machine.

Meanwhile infantrymen were swimming near the ship in their heavy overcoats and with their tommy guns gripped by straps between their teeth. German fighter planes flew twenty-five feet above them, using their machine guns and aiming at those wearing forage caps.

From the shore I could see men in the water smiling with a sort of joyful desperation. Some would sink silently. The whole thing was so calculated, slow-moving, and orderly that its horror was intensified a hundredfold.

Pale, worn-out men clambered on to the shore, cleaned their rifles, stripped off their coats, and at once fell in for roll call. Some of them would run back into the water to gather the floating caps of the dead. Part of the ship blew up when fire reached the ammunition in the hold. A bright streak of flame, followed by deep-blue smoke, billowed out from below its decks.

Deck planks which had been hurled into the air crashed down, wounding survivors. The crew remained on board. The explosion in the hold had blocked the door to the mess room, where there were wounded lying. Burning fuel was flowing from the engine room along a gangway. This leaked through the mess-room door. It could not be stopped. Engulfed in the burning liquid, wounded men struggled to get through portholes, but these were too narrow for their shoulders. Escape was impossible. These wounded men were not armed and could not kill themselves. A sailor struggled along the deck outside, to the porthole through which the head of an agonized friend appeared. His comrade begged him to kill him. The sailor drew his revolver and fired. He then slid the revolver down the deck and turned away. He had done what he could. He had helped his friend.

" Abandon ship," was ordered over the loud-speaker. The men jumped overboard. The captain, the commissar, and the mate fixed daggers in their belts. Death has its discipline. They roped themselves to the railing of the bridge. Then from the shore came the order: " Officers to leave ship." Lives are valuable in Sevastopol. In the water the chief officer and the captain had between them the commissar, who had lost both hands in the Civil War.

The last moment had come. The decks were awash and seas were breaking over the lofty anti-aircraft post. Here women gunners, in uniforms of Marines, were still operating their guns, trying to keep the fighters away from our men in the sea. We could hear their voices. " Vainly the old woman waits for the return of her son," they were singing. The flag was struck. Then the gunners clambered on to the guns and plunged into the waves. That was all. Suddenly the ship's siren, long and doleful, was heard. Who sounded that last salute to the deathless women of Sevastopol?

The vessel went down, but her survivors were not willing to go to the Admiralty. They did not want to eat or sleep. They wanted to fight and were sent straight in to an attack. They went for the Germans with hands and teeth so that in the morning hundreds of torn, bloodstained bodies of the enemy were left on front-line positions. The " Black Death," as the Germans call the Russian Marines, had once again taken revenge.

It was now evening. The setting sun threw its golden glow on the ruins. Through the streets walked an old woman, followed by a boy staggering with a bucket of yellow paint. With a big brush and in clumsy lettering she wrote on ruins: " Death, death to you Germans. Die, you Germans! Die! "

Nobody had ordered her to do this. It was her own idea.

At the turn of a road a wine shop was damaged. Drivers were dragging away a lorry of red wine, which slopped over its side.

Marines were rolling gigantic safes from the ruined State Bank and turning them into massive barricades across a street.

Perched on top of the single remaining wall of a four-storey building, a man held binoculars to his eyes. He was charting every new explosion, and informing staff headquarters as buildings collapsed.

Members of volunteer rescue squads with shovels and levers were on their way to dig for the imprisoned and to rescue State property. A girl ran out of a cellar. Her dress was on fire. A man ran to a water tub. "Don't touch it. Throw me in," the girl cried.

Some one bent over a delayed-action bomb. Puffing and panting, he was trying to unscrew the fuse. Angrily he sat on the mine to get leverage on his wrench.

Here are two schoolgirls who have crept fifteen miles. They are dusty, grimy, scratched with stones and shell splinters, covered with blisters ; and their legs are bruised. They have made seventy-two repairs to a damaged telephone cable. Several girls set out on this perilous job, but these two are the only ones to return and their young cheeks are smeared with tear-stains for their school friends.

At Malakhov Kurgan stood a lorry unloading anti-aircraft guns. We were passed by a line of women carrying buckets wrapped in towels. In the buckets there was borsht. They were taking food to the front line. What worried them most was how to keep the borsht hot. They vanished behind white Inkerman-stone buildings. We went into the quarters of the town defence committee, the effective local government of the besieged city. In one big room active committee members were having their wounds bandaged, switchboard girls were calling monotonous hello's, arms were being handed out to the mobilized, advice was being given, instructions read, while one man was having a tooth extracted. In a corner tommy guns were being issued. " That is better. Now

I feel more comfortable," one man said, and taking a knife from his pocket, he began to carve his name on its butt. He put a few doves round it as a decoration. They flew as gaily as if the war were over.

Behind him was a line of girls from the Regional Soviet, from macaroni factories—group leaders of the Pioneer movement. One after another passed the table where once they used to get official forms or bundles of pamphlets. Today they got tommy guns. There were no farewells or speeches. That was out of fashion.

At a large handsome dining-table, supported by massive brass mermaids, there sat a fat, gruff-voiced man who was sweating from lack of air and the violence of his own language. He was chief of the ammonal explosive stores, to whose rough hands—he was formerly a Sevastopol gardener—was entrusted the entire supply of explosives for the city. He looked after the explosives as tenderly as though they were roses. Facing him across the magnificent table crowded the directors of various local enterprises whose factories and workshops lay on the edge of the defences. In the event of a break-through by the enemy, they were ordered to blow up everything. No one was satisfied with what the prudent gardener issued. " Why so stingy? It is not for concrete or timber we are asking. We built these places ourselves and know very well how much is needed to demolish them," they say querulously.

The gardener is obstinate. He knows the extent of his stock and is afraid he will not have enough when they are really needed. As he rejected one manager's application, he said: " What, do you expect me to have to blow up all your factories? Why, I haven't enough for my own hothouse." So the factory directors laughingly went off to do something they had never expected.

Soon they would be laying explosives under what many of them held dearest in life. But not one of them believed he would ever have to light the fuses. Only with a joke, as the gardener wisely understood, could anybody do such terrible work.

Next to the explosives merchant, there was a girl with a pretty little nose, and plaits, and a bright-green ribbon round her head. She had new high-heeled shoes on, for the first time apparently, for they squeaked. She looked immensely pleased with herself.

She was the daughter of one of the members of the town defence committee. Now in her big schoolgirl handwriting, she was keeping the town register. " I registered two marriages today," she told me. " Besides I entered one new-born baby. It was brought from the Crimean Mountains, where the partisans are. I asked Daddy to let me go there, but he won't. The baby's mother, who is nursing it, had the right to leave the partisans by plane for the ' Big Land,' but she did not want to leave, so the pilot took the baby alone, with milk and a comforter. Did you know that the secretary of the Comsomol is growing a moustache. He is thin, but he works all right. What a fool I am! I don't know if I really like fat men. Today he gave me new figures of the Comsomol participation in these heroic days. Fifteen hundred of them have joined the Army. I asked Father again whether I could go, but he said no. If I had gone I could have written down fifteen hundred and one, which is a more convincing figure, because Daddy said at the Centre that he did not like round figures. Pioneers and Comsomols have filled a hundred and fifty thousand anti-tank liquid bottles. The same girls have made thousands of grenades. I asked Father again to let me go and work with them. I am not afraid. They collected two tons of scrap and half a ton of tin cans. I never saw the cans. It would be interesting to see how it all looked.

"For the tank *Tanya* there was collected a hundred thousand rubles. Such a pity! We collected it, and the pilot took it all away. Why didn't they send me with it? I would have given it straight to Stalin myself. I am sure he would have shaken my hand, and if he had asked me to stay for tea I would have told him all about Father. We have trained five hundred chauffeurs and six thousand Red Cross workers.

"I asked to be a nurse. Father wouldn't allow me. In place of those who had left, the Comsomols took in five thousand new members. Three girls—Vanda, Olga, and Tanya—got medals. I have seen them myself. They are so stuck-up. Now I want a medal so much. Anyway, I will do something and either they will kick me out or decorate me."

Then this girl thought about her mother and cried. She looked at her father and began to read a summary of statistics. And then she rewrote it, making a clean copy for the chairman as she would in school for her teacher.

Beside her a man with a bandaged head said: "Is it clear why we need substitutes?" "Quite—to take our places if killed," replied an old man with a fox-like face. "Right." "Who will take your place?" "I am his substitute," said his wife; "God is merciful and wouldn't kill me for my sufferings." When she said "sufferings" she looked reproachfully at her husband. The old man was a foreman in an important department. His wife was a strong woman who had spent most of her life beside him in the factory. She knew her husband's weakness, that he liked to drink. So she had stood over him day and night and willy-nilly learned his job in the factory.

With their savings she had built a small house at Zhem-chuzhnaya Harbour. Its whitewashed walls were prettily outlined against the blue background of the bay. Every time she went back there with her husband, she would say: "Look, my lad, there is your vodka," and point to their house. Now their home was just a heap of ruins.

A short meeting was being held in a corner. A man with a thoughtful, gentle face said: "All pregnant women are immediately to evacuate. The third offensive has begun. The first fighting is at the Mæcenas Mountains and Balaklava. You must begin at once. The Germans did not advance a step in their first two offensives, which cost them 70,000 wounded and 20,000 killed. They have promised their men to enter the city in three days. By that time they will have lost 150,000 men. Let's talk about town matters. Why are you sitting there? I said: start evacuating. And take this down: 'Reference: Future preparations of population for armed fighting within the city.'"

That was how everybody found out about the third offensive. The people felt relieved when they heard it. Most of them smiled. Somebody snapped a cigarette-case noisily and said: "So the curtain is up. The première has begun." He then went to a typist, sat down, and started to dictate a leading article for his paper. "I am working out ideas," he said; "Anna Alexeevna, we must say 'Not a step back.' We should not write about ourselves as 'tortured by the Fascists,' damn them, we have got to kill these murderers, and that is why 'not a step back' is better. Anna typed.

Outside, it was beginning to grow dark. At this moment Sevastopol was fighting on many fronts. The belt of the coastal artillery was reflected in the sea by thousands of bright sparks. As night fell, the batteries grew more active. During the day, except for certain of them, they were usually quiet in order not to betray their positions to the enemy's reconnaissance planes and also to surprise him should he attempt a landing.

The naval gunners worked energetically and did miracles, modestly but smartly and quickly, as they sent death to the enemy. The battery where I stood was a model of order and efficiency. Something fell suddenly in the clay. It was the head of a dead man with brain, blood, bone, and hair oozing from it. A new man took his place, and as he came forward he slipped and nearly fell on the bloody mess. " What is the matter today, Pavel? Why can't you be more careful? " said the major who was present at this scene. " It won't happen again, major. It is the last time," the corporal replied, as evenly as if his superior were giving him a decoration.

In the eastern sky, behind the Chernaya River, a whole section blazed, and outlined against it stood a dense column of smoke, broadening as it rose. To me, it seemed more elemental than any volcano, this man-made catastrophe.

At night the Sevastopol sky was ours. Germany's best night pilots lay drowned under the wreckage of their planes below the waters of the Bay. As soon as dusk drew its veil over the throbbing battlefield, our planes set out to avenge the day's destruction. Signals winked on an airfield, motors roared, and bombers, Stormaviks, and fighters, even training planes, set off on the first of many flights to bomb the enemy's first-line positions. The front was near and many flights were made nightly.

It was easier in the night to walk through the city. Upon reaching the ruined entrance to the historic museum, housing the Roubaud Panorama, I entered through a shell-hole. Here had been a superb reconstruction of the defence of Sevastopol on June 6, 1855. Today it was June 6, 1942.

Though the walls of the museum were damaged, they still stood, but the glass-domed roof had fallen and slivers of glass had slashed the painting. The flicker of distant fires, breaking in through the gaping roof, illuminated the scene faintly and revealed sections of the great Panorama—the Andreyev and the Vladimir banners,* ships' figureheads, and desperate charges.

As I stood there silent and tense, feeling myself under the scrutiny of those historical figures which loomed out of the darkness, a hoarse voice broke in: " What do you want, young man? The museum is closed." A figure stepped forward and I recognized the curator. He was a thin old man with a bandaged throat. With him were two wounded Red Army men on crutches. One of them turned to the old fellow and said: " Perhaps you will tell us something about this place. Because of our wounds we are being sent to a hospital in the ' Big Land.' We've heard about this museum, but have never seen it. We have been at the front the whole time."

" The museum is closed," the old man replied.

" Don't worry, we will pay," said the second wounded man, who had a peasant's face and thick beard.

" I don't want your money, soldiers, I have plenty."

" So you get your wages although the place is damaged? "

" I don't need wages. I live on what I get for my killed sons."

" For how many? " one soldier asked, as if being paid " for the killed " was the old man's regular normal profession.

* The Andreyev banner is the Imperial Russian nautical ensign, showing the Cross of St. Andrew. The Vladimir banner is the flag of the Vladimir regiment, which defended Sevastopol during the Crimean War.

" Four—four," the guide replied. " One was killed in the Finnish War, one was missing at Khalkin-gol,* and the other two were drowned at Feodosia."

" Any grandchildren? " asked the bearded infantryman.

" Yes. Two."

" That means your children are still alive. Don't worry, it is all right so long as the family goes on. The war combs out everybody, you know."

This idea seemed to touch the old man, for after a little reflection he said: " Very well. Only you will have to excuse me if I forget a few things. I have not been round for a long time."

" *Nitchevo!* Never mind! We are not trying to catch you. Just tell us the truth," said the bearded man.

In the centre of the round hall we piled broken furniture and made a bonfire which lit its walls. Settling down to listen, the wounded soldiers sat near the fire on a gun carriage, occasionally using the crutches to stir its embers.

The lecture began: " This painting was created by the famous artist Roubaud. It is 495 feet in length and 49 feet high."

" Leave that out," said the soldiers.

" But these are not heroes you see, but deluded professional soldiers who were thrown unwillingly into the war. When you look at the faces of men who passed on twenty-five years ago, you see the training of Nicholas's army. . . ." The old man was reading from a Crimean guide book which had been written by some idiot in 1935.

" Please tell us something about the pictures, without the book. It will be more interesting," the soldiers begged. Once the old fellow had laid aside the guide book, things went better. He was a wonderful talker,

* The site, on the Manchurian-Mongolian border, of the greatest battle of the undeclared war between Soviet and Japanese troops, in the summer of 1939, which resulted in the total defeat of the Japanese.

and knew Sevastopol's history profoundly and intelligently. As he talked he used old-fashioned phrases which infused all that he said with that special character of sturdy solemnity, that truly Russian quality. Sevastopol he called, for instance, "Fiery Golgotha," and when he told about the city's last days he said: "And if then no tears flowed it was because no one was left to shed them. And those hearts which had been tender had been hardened in the fire which had blazed so long in the city."

Pointing to a group of soldiers who were being bandaged by beautiful Sisters of Mercy, he said: "The deeds of Sevastopol's people were so divine, rare, and singular that their grandchildren are incredulous and bewildered by their bravery, which grew with danger and surprised even our enemies."

In referring to the cowardly behaviour of one of the Allies' artillery batteries, he delicately said: "Their field artillery found itself under the necessity of having to run away as quickly as possible." As he recalled Sevastopol's early history, he led us to the damaged wall, and pointing into the darkness, he said: "Here is Malakhov Kurgan. Long ago a tavern stood there and in that tavern there lived an old naval captain who was a famous drunkard, but a practical man. He was Malakhov. When the Admiralty wanted a skipper it sent a messenger for him with the words: 'Run over to Malakhov Kurgan.' Later the name was changed to Kornilov Kurgan. . . . And here," said the old man pointing at a gaping shell-hole, "is the Georgievsky Monastery. In ancient times it was a temple to Diana in which priestesses worshipped Agamemnon's daughter."

"That is where our Marines are now, a suitable place for them," one of the soldiers interrupted.

"On the other side of Quarantine Harbour," the old

man went on, " is Chersonese-Tauricus, which was celebrated long ago for its wealth, trade, and possessions. It was founded 600 years before Christ. In 988 Grand Duke Vladimir of Russia seized Chersonese and was baptized there."

" Yes, we have been there," the soldiers added. " We caught two parachutists there . . . the fat Fritzies ran like cats."

A new day dawned. The fire went out. We left the ruined museum. Pointing towards Balaklava, the old man continued : " Long ago Balaklava was a pirates' harbour. Two thousand years before Christ, on the way to Colchis, Jason stopped there to smoke them out of their nest."

" The scoundrels are there still," said the bearded soldier. " We will do something about them without Jason's help."

" Do you see that white Chersonese Lighthouse? It was called the Cape of the Virgin. There lay the virgin forest of Diana and on the cape were the sacrificial altars of the gods. People were sacrificed there by the priestesses."

" A hell of a business," muttered one of the wounded men. " You have studied this well, old man. You know everything. Our best thanks. Would you care to drink with us? "

The old man refused. His eyes were full of tears, for his reminiscences had shaken him to his soul. He asked us to help him throw into the cellar all that remained of the Panorama properties and we did. The sandbags which were the Panorama's bastions, lines of shell-cases, the wheels of gun carriages, stuffed horses, everything that remained at the foot of the walls we gathered up and flung into the cellar.

The dawning sky was still starlit. Gigantic columns of smoke were rising, and from afar there was a terrifying rumble of cannonade. Against the brightening horizon stood outlined such of the buildings of Sevastopol as had miraculously escaped. Lenin with his compelling outstretched arm, standing firm and secure among the wreckage of the city, called on all to whom the honour of Sevastopol and the Motherland were dear to equal or surpass the glorious deeds of the first Sevastopol defence.

Motionless and silent before this indescribable spectacle, all thoughts and feelings expelled by its horror, we gazed as we had often looked out to sea at oncoming storms. The old man, remembering something important, raised his hoarse voice: " Long live Christianity—" He did not finish his story. A Junkers, above us, dived. Guns spoke. Another day had begun.

CHAPTER IX

THE day was dazzlingly bright and hot. On such days before the war you would have seen dozens of yachts on the horizon. Today, over the calm, taut surface of the sea a mist crept from the salt marshes. By screwing up your eyes and looking steadily at the horizon, you could see mirages. Shaggy camels wandered across the sea, and from the mist rose fantastic palaces and castles— magical and surprising. But unless you kept your eyes screwed up and moved your head slowly from side to side, the camels and castles vanished.

The Last Days

A grey-haired lad, lost in thought, sat on the beach beside the sleeping sea. Marines had brought him here. They had cleared a place for him by the sea—lifted him on to a pile of rocks so that he could see around him better, for he loved the sea, though now it was forbidden to him.

He could not walk. His feet had been burned and pierced through by bayonets. This the Germans had done. They had caught him at a moment when he was loaded with Skoda tommy guns, staff documents in shiny patent-leather files, and bright-coloured maps marked with figures and lines as he was returning home from his twelfth reconnaissance raid of the month.

He was not a reconnaissance officer, but he answered the Germans with the revengeful rage of a man. For he remembered very clearly the moment when suddenly there had entered his room armed men who had talked a strange language and had dared to strip his mother. They called it " searching." They undressed his mother carefully and slowly. A tall, thin man with thick spectacles took her dress and stockings and laid them precisely on a chair. Then they attentively scrutinized the boy's mother. She covered her face with her hands as she stood nude against a wall.

They left the boy in the room all the time. Two men with stripes on their sleeves came to her, took her in turn on their knees, and embraced her while a third took photographs. She did not resist. She knew what to expect from these people. They could kill her son. Then they pushed her on to a bed. She took her hands from her face and bit somebody's hands deep to the bone. In the grip of anger, the boy jumped at the soldiers. A lieutenant pushed him away and said: " Little fool. That is the way you were made." There were many Germans.

When they left, the boy covered his mother with a blanket. Her face was wet, but she no longer wept. It was the sweat and tears of a dead woman.

The boy turned grey. When the Marines retreated from Nikolayev, they took him along. They gave him the uniform and weapons of a dead man. With these he passed Perekop Isthmus, fighting beside them in the heavy moments of tank attacks, standing by them during the winter and spring warfare in the trenches, defending Sevastopol, which he had never seen.

Twice when wounded he was given sick leave. War ages children. Quickly he had learned to crawl, to throw grenades, to use captured rifles, to go long without food when raiding, and to play the Tyrolean march on a mouth organ. It was by fooling about with the Tyrolean march that he let the stupid Westphalians capture him in the front lines. One morning, after a dark night full of fearsome noise, when he had been working his way through barbed wire, avoiding a mine field by clambering from tree to tree and passing hundreds of death traps, the Germans caught him. Without hesitating he said: " Hello, I am a kulak's son." But this time the officer did not believe him, for he had been taken red-handed. " Crucify this brave Russian boy," the officer said. It was not a joke. They crucified him. Of course, they would not have done it if he had told them what he knew, but he had kept silent. They piled wood under his feet and set it afire. The wooden cross, which caught fire at its base, fell on him. The Germans thought him dead.

At night our Marines went to look for him. They beat off two attacks and dragged the cross back to their trench. The boy, who was alive, was said to have gone quite white.

The old sailor who looked after the cripple was a

veteran of sixty years with the Black Sea Navy. During the siege of Sevastopol he approached the Marines and asked to be " in the business." But he was not allowed " in the business " though everybody respected him as a sailor who had served under Lieutenant Schmidt on the mutinous *Potemkin** at Odessa, and even though he knew the old, forgotten songs of the sea.

At night with a trembling cracked bass voice he used to sing "On the bottom of Sevastopol Bay lies the warship *Maria*." The men listened intently. But they would not take him in their attacks, so the old man took to making envelopes. Ingeniously he used scissors to cut out most wonderfully ornamental envelopes which, to do them justice were worthy to have been carried in troikas with bells as postchaises.

These filigree envelopes brought him great fame. He was the best-known and respected man in the brigade. And it was he who was ordered to look after the boy. He was an old ship's surgeon, with little faith in doctors and his first medical principle was " to get the rust out of a wound with pus."

Today was the first day that the boy had been brought out into the fresh air, and together this white-headed pair sat on the beach. As he cut out envelopes, the old man gently ventured: " Now, young man, there is this business about parents. It is no good, having no parents. Parents there have got to be. We must put this matter in order." The boy opened his eyes wide and quietly replied: " One aunty whom I do not know said she would be my mother." " All right," said the old man ; " a mother, even if she is a new one, is absolutely necessary. This is enough for today, let's go into the shelter.

* A battleship seized by revolutionaries in the late summer of 1905. It terrorized the Black Sea until forced to seek internment in Rumania. The mutiny was short but impressive.

We might scorch your wounds in the sun. Come on, you Marines, help the lad home." The Marines came over. Carefully lifting the boy from the pile of rocks, they carried him into the trenches. The sea was calm. The mist had vanished. The castles and camels had gone down to the bottom of the Black Sea.

By chance I happened to be present at the investigation of a remarkable event. The story was told by the commander of the Marines. Formerly a helmsman, he had the high, pronounced cheek-bones of an Asiatic, and piercing screwed-up eyes—a tough character, the sort that would make a man jump on sight. His speech was slow and deliberate, as if revealing his thought for a second time. As he talked he clenched and unclenched his fists and brought them down heavily on the table to give added emphasis to his words.

The tale he had to tell was so terrifying that I have tried hard to forget it. He told it in a natural, precise manner. At first my squeamishness resisted. The way he went into anatomical details I took to be bravado, for I had often noticed that it is the habit of cowards to give an impression of toughness in this way. But as his report continued, it gripped my attention. I noticed that the man was not posing but simply describing with professional care and exactitude the place and circumstance of a crime. And as one dreadful detail followed another, my indignation grew, and I was filled with hatred for the scoundrel when he was eventually conducted in by a sentry.

This is a softened form of the story told by the commander. It is written approximately as he gave it:

" Before this trench, about twenty yards away from this place, is a piece of land for the possession of which a battle was fought for seven months and eighteen days. In the communiqués it was known as a front-line position. One's imagination boggles at the way in which the living and the dead jostle one another all along this narrow front. In the last ten days the Germans lost 211 planes there. General von Mannstein's army numbered about 280,000, and that was on a front of less than thirty miles. Up to yesterday we routed 148,000 of them, including Rumanians, and killed about 60,000. The dead were carefully counted, otherwise you do not get reserves. The unlucky ones then, with ours, numbering some 90,000 were rotting. The heat accelerates that process. If you will climb up the nearest little hill, and have good eyesight, you will see that narrow sector between the German trenches and our lines covered with decaying corpses. The bodies are several layers deep, and in some places are piled up to a man's height, which only shows that there were more attacks here than elsewhere.

" A corporal estimated the number of attacks by the depth of the unburied dead before the lines. The ground around here absorbs blood badly, so it has to find its way through rock in the way that rain-water does. All the rest that comes out of a body besides blood forms a stinking mess. The maggoty filth reaches the trenches so that men trample on it underfoot. The most energetic steps we take against it cannot overcome the process of decay. Lime cannot keep up with it. Thousands of new dead are added every day. Now the stench is choking. Sometimes the strongest of us faint. Nothing can be done about it. It is the smell of war, and those who think it smells otherwise are mistaken. You are lucky today, as the wind is from the sea. If we could keep it that way and send all this stink towards the Mikensevy Mountains we should suffocate the Germans, but that, I am

102

afraid, is only fantasy. What we are talking about is reality.

"Three days ago, just before dawn, we noticed that some of the dead were sitting in a circle facing outwards. No, it wasn't a hallucination. We heard them talking and, it seemed, arguing with each other. Apart from this group others sat in pairs. A particularly strange effect was made by one of our sailors, who sat leaning towards a headless German with his arms raised to the moon. At his feet lay his helmet, with a mess of fresh brains dribbling over its edge ; and his tunic was bunched up above his chest. The others were balanced on all fours or in obscene embraces. Some of them seemed to be smiling with torn mouths and distorted faces ; some lay on their sides as if sun-bathing, or with their arms stretched out as if practising swimming strokes. The worst was one with a smashed stomach and chest. All that had been inside lay in his lap under his hands and it looked as if the dead man was trying to shove his guts back again. He looked at us with protruding eyes.

"During the siege we have seen many things. Last December, on Height 615, the Germans took the most severely wounded of our Marines and arranged them in the shape of swastikas. Then they poured petrol on them and set them on fire. All night that blazing star lit up the valley. I remember as in a dream, two sisters who were impaled, with their long hair floating in the wind and shameful words beneath their feet. But this circus of the dead was worse than any of those things in a nightmare. Early in the morning we noted that some of the soldiers' pockets were turned inside out and that others were naked.

"Who could have defiled and insulted the dead in this way? It was clear there was a thief—a German thief.

Someone was after gold teeth, a silver cigarette-case or a pipe. The scoundrel worked at night.

" When the sun had risen we could not face the horror. At night death had been dreadful and strange; the day-light exposed their staring wounds and the indecency of their poses and gestures.

" Someone in the German trenches was howling hysterically. Many of us were beside ourselves, too. The machine-gunners fired a burst and the dead fell again. A headless figure was the most stubborn. Someone threw a grenade. Its arms dropped and it toppled forward to the ground.

" Next night the same thing happened again. We were in a rage and decided to ambush. Planks were thrown across from body to body so that our men could creep forward to within thirty yards of the German lines. Here they lay as if dead.

" The moon rose. Towards us, glancing fearfully from side to side, crept a man. Stumbling and slithering and sometimes gripping corpses to support himself, he talked to the dead as he approached. We could not understand what he was saying. He came to us quickly enough and we saw that he wore a diver's rubber overall. I felt his breath on my neck, his hand in my pocket, and then I jumped up and shouted. The man screamed and fell in terror. Now he is here. Listen to him."

The investigation had just started. The matter was quite clear. Everybody understood that the procedure was only a formality before the carrying-out of sentence. However, an instructor of the Political Department, who was examining a criminal for the first time in his life, could not let the opportunity slip of demonstrating his talents. Everybody was angry and impatient, for they knew that the procedure was unnecessary, but that did not hinder the instructor from assuming that somehow it was his business—his " political part."

I looked for the captured scoundrel. In a corner of a dimly-lit dugout stood a Russian sailor. Not a German but a Russian—one of ours. I could not see his face. One leg in the sailor's loose trousers was placed decisively forward. Behind, leaning against the wall, two giants were just visible. They were breathing heavily. The examiner sat at a simple table sipping a glass of muddy tea and slowly cleaning his pipe, putting the ashes into an inkstand. Then he got up and said: " Why are you hiding yourself, gravedigger? You are used to working at night, eh? Afraid of the light? Come out in the open. We shall talk with you in Remula Roma language."

Nobody in the room knew what he meant by " Remula Roma language " and we thought that it must be some esoteric mystery known only to those who had reached the zenith of judicial refinement. The grunting giants pushed the sailor forward a little, and now I could see his face. His eyes were half-closed, his lips were compressed, the muscles of his cheeks were twitching, his forehead was deeply wrinkled, and his bushy eyebrows slanted steeply, giving him an expression of suffering and astonishment.

The accused put his hands in his pockets and stood motionless without change of expression until the investigation was over. While the accusation was being read, there was one phrase which he repeated several times: " Allow me to report—" And then he stopped dead, for the examiner refused him an opportunity " to report."

This sailor, who stood so firmly with one leg resolutely forward did not look at us, but maintained a scornful, supercilious expression. I now saw him clearly and found some of the traces of his terrible profession in his appearance, but there was something else there, too, which I could not explain to myself.

" Rank? "

" Bosun."

" Unit? "

" I am from the next brigade."

" So you are not a native? "

" No, not from this place."

The helmsman interrupted to say that the accused man's commissar had been sent for and would arrive shortly.

" Thanks," said the bosun merrily. " The matter is not worth a kopek ; not worth wasting the paper on it. May I please report, Comrade Commissar? "

" I will give you comrade, you damned thief. What sort of comrade do you think I am to you? Stand still. Are you crazy? "

" Not at all. I am in excellent health," the bosun answered insolently.

" Then answer as the law requires."

" But may I report? "

" What was the meaning of your talking to the dead? "

" I was talking to myself, Comrade Commander. It was rather frightening out there with all the dead about and not a living soul around."

" Frightening? It would have been better for you if you had been a spy rather than a villain doing such a thing to your dead comrades. Why did you do it, eh? Answer, hyena."

The " hyena " advanced to the table, opened his eyes wide, and for the first time looked angrily at the instructor.

" I have lived forty-three years, let me tell you, and

106

nobody has ever called me a hyena before, even in the czarist days. I didn't do it. It was the Germans. Let me report."

"Turn out your pockets. We shall see how much truth there is in what you say."

The bosun, who had been holding himself under such tight control, suddenly slackened.

"Turn them out or we will help you."

"Don't touch me. I will do it myself," he said to the giants behind him.

While he was emptying his pockets, the commander, who had been watching him closely all the time, turned to the instructor and asked him what he thought of the case.

"Thief."

"What else?"

"Demoralization and a bad political standard in his unit."

"What else?"

"A desire to benefit from the helpless condition of his dead comrades."

"Is that all?"

"Execution."

"Nothing more?"

"I am not a Dostoyevsky to dig into this filth."

"I see. But I think there is a certain kind of bravery in this man's action. He is degraded, but brave. If it could be directed another way, nobody knows whether he or you would prove to be the better man."

The bosun had laid on the table all the contents of his pockets. There lay letters, a cap, badges, medals, scraps of trousers and jerseys, torn notebooks, Navy ribbons, buttons, and the like.

"Where are the money, the cigarette-holders and

watches? You have thrown them away, eh? Don't try to fool me with that junk."

"It is not junk," the bosun replied, growing red with anger and clenching his fists.

"That is hardly treasure."

"Maybe it is more than that."

"You are getting impertinent," said the instructor, taking a revolver in his hand.

"I don't know what it is to you, but for the wives, children, and relatives of the dead, these scraps are the dearest things in the world because they are all that is left to them of the men who died for their country. For such a piece of cloth or this blood-stained photograph, let alone the letters, there are women who would give their lives, and when they have ceased weeping, they will wear them next to their hearts all their lives. And, I ask you to consider, Citizen Judge, that a Russian man, though he be in the Army, honours and respects the memory of the dead. We in our village were little boys when we were photographed beside our father's coffin, though it cost us our last penny. If a man knows he will not be forgotten after he is dead, and that his wife and children will learn the truth and be consoled by someone who sends them a letter about his last minutes, or a souvenir, then he won't be afraid of attack. When I saw that the Germans had lost their fear when they went out to rob the dead, I asked myself why it was that I hadn't the spunk to go out there and do something useful, and I got ashamed and angry with myself and went. For two days it was all right. Then I was caught."

"That is all?" asked the embarrassed instructor.

"No, not yet," the bosun answered. "I see you are an infantryman and I know it is hard for you to understand a sailor. I sailed the seas with these dead men for years.

I have gone down into the seas with them, have been on one ship with them for six years, and that was why for the sake of this junk, as you called it, it was easy to rip the fear out of my heart."

The bosun stopped. The commander picked up an open envelope which was lying on the table, took out a letter and a copper buckle that was engraved with an anchor and a note. He read aloud: "And so, dear Ksenya Mikailovna, I am sending you the buckle from Petka's belt—pass it down from generation to generation because it can serve as a symbol for his deeds at Sevastopol."

At this moment the door opened and the commissar of the bosun's unit came into the dugout.

" What, caught again? " he said.

" Exactly," answered the bosun.

" Smart fellow. Are you ready for reconnaissance now? Go wash yourself, you stink."

" Yes, I will. It was not exactly like picking apples."

The embarrassed instructor hastily left the dugout. The bosun cheered up, put all the scrap into his pockets, and left with the commissar.

I went with the commander on to a height which commanded a view of everything. There was no wind from the sea now. After five minutes I began to vomit. What I saw was far worse than the commander's story. I stayed eight minutes for the sake of decency ; then, telling him that I was busy, I went hastily to the car.

CHAPTER X

THE front ran from the Balaklava Mountains to the smooth North Side of the bay. On peaks above Balaklava there were still perched partly ruined Genoese forts. As a child I saw these ruins for the first time in company with some unknown and most inquisitive Germans. They were equipped with Finnish hunting knives, cameras, maps, and compasses ; they drank our wine from their hunting flasks, sang bawdy student songs, and scratched their initials in Gothic characters on the mossy stones of the old museum.

And here, at Balaklava, we were meeting again—grown up. Maybe they were different Germans from those tourists, but for me all Germans were much the same.

There were Alpine Jäger troops in the Genoese towers ; the old pirate cave now sheltered bandits from the Tyrol. We who were below controlled all the land fringing the little bay. Wind howled round the forts. It was never still there, and even when it was quite calm in the harbour, you could hear the whistling above. At this season it blew strong at sunset.

Before the enemy came, tame birds which used to live in the towers would come sweeping out on the breeze. But the day that I was there it was a cloud of leaflets that floated out of the embrasures in the ancient walls. They drifted over Balaklava and were tossed by the clashing winds, which dropped some into the sea and some on the land. Apparently they were in reply to a poster which we had put up the day before, on the face of the cliff right in front of the Germans: " Fritz, the gold of the *Black Prince* is waiting for you on the bottom of Balaklava Bay. **Hurry up.**"

One that fell near me was not a leaflet but a page from a pornographic magazine. I trained my binoculars on the tower. A number of Germans were standing on the edge of the cliff shaking their fists, apparently, at the fellow who had unwittingly launched on the wind a parcel which was intended for German instead of Russian reading. I saw one fat man backing nervously away from the others —the angry subscribers. Beside me stood a sailor. He looked through the magazine, spat, and said: " Yes, that is the way these foxy snakes come into the world," tore it up, and threw it into the harbour.

Four hours before, the Germans had begun to descend, trying to seize the port. Their plan, which was not well conceived, failed. But at the other end of the front things were worse, for there they had come out on the North Side. That was the first serious break-through of the third offensive. On the Sevastopol front every yard was the equivalent of far greater length on another front. From an aeroplane you could see how the continuous curved line of the front, with each end in the sea, bulged and straightened out as attack succeeded counter-attack. Immediately behind the defenders, as well as deep in the rear, were the waters of the vast Black Sea. Behind the attackers—the boundless Ukrainian steppe, the Crimea, across which reinforcements were streaming ceaselessly.

Just before dawn our right flank had become quiet; artillery fire was sporadic. All the gorges and cliffs in the hills, the slopes of which were covered with dusty scrub, sank into an uneasy calm. The battle was shifting northwards from the Balaklava sectors. Once again the Marines had held the enemy. Now he was trying to pierce through to the city on a neighbouring sector. If he met the same resistance there, he would bound back. For ten days now, covered by hundreds of planes, many long-distance guns, and formidable tanks, he had swung from sector to sector, from North Side to Balaklava and back, probing for a weak spot in the defence.

He had all the advantages of manœuverability, and was able to concentrate great pressure on the principal sectors by borrowing strength for long or brief periods from those of secondary importance. For us such tactics were impossible, for to weaken any one sector would mean to risk the catastrophe of a break-through. We must be able to repulse any blow at every point.

The eastern sky lightened— the eleventh day of the offensive dawned. The night watch was relieved—stars grew dim amid the shell-bursts. The squadrons of vessels which had reached the coast during the night had vanished into the mist, pursued by shells of all calibres.

The loud-speakers fell silent. Each side made use of this form of propaganda, and when night fell a regular radio duel began. Actually it was more of a scramble than a duel—a scrambling fight among announcers, drivers, and gunners. Heavily armoured radio vans would dash wildly from valley to valley trying to avoid the gunfire that would be directed at them as they gave their positions away by their sound. The announcers would compete not only in volume but in the presentation of their material. Each talked the enemy's language— we, German and Rumanian ; they, Russian. The announcers came to know each other well during the siege and loudly reproached each other for professional faults, for bad grammar, poor jokes, traces of drunkenness in their voices, and other technical shortcomings. These exchanges of personalities were highly popular in the trenches, and every time the quips and the cracks of our announcer were heard, roars of laughter would be audible from the German trenches.

German propaganda broadcasts on the Sevastopol front were largely for the Navy. Their transmission would begin with an appeal to the Marines—of whom the Germans were most afraid. The end would usually begin something like this: " You who bear the name of ' Black Death,' awaken from your opium dream of Bolshevist propaganda. A German sailor is talking to you. I have the same feelings as you. If you love the Black Sea, come to us and it will be yours as before. Our Führer will appreciate your action and give each of you a motor launch." Our men would roar with laughter, and our radio people cleverly transmitted the laughter back to the Germans. Once our loud-speaker put on a laughter record for fifty minutes following a particularly ridiculous statement by the enemy. The Germans opened up with gunfire and switched on their sirens, trying to drown out the laughter, but in vain. The mockery echoed in the hills and swept over their lines, filling the night with ghoulish and fearful sounds.

In a lorry which had been used to convey the dead from the front, we reached the Marine headquarters. Beside a doctor from the medical staff sat a girl. On her cheek was a large roughly sewn scar ; her hands were torn and filthy ; over her right ear her hair was burned. There was blood dripping from one of her boots. Despite its grime and greenish pallor, her face had traces of great beauty. She bore signs of complete exhaustion. With her chin resting against a tommy gun, she gazed with wide-open eyes at the hills. The medical worker was counting dead, calculating the total of the past twenty-four hours. It was no easy job that this prematurely bald young man had—the collection and disposal of the dead in his sector.

At this moment this " Chief of the Immortality Department," as the Marines called him, had finished his calculations and had resumed an attempted flirtation which had begun by her somewhat unfortunately thus:

" Why are you laughing so unpleasantly? Your work is far from being funny, I should imagine."

" Three hours of hearty laughter is equal in calories to two eggs."

" You would have done better to have eaten two eggs."

" I see that you are a woman, after all, though you are dirty enough to be a soldier."

" I am a soldier. If I had been a woman I would not have said a word to you."

The confused but indignant medical worker rose unsteadily and clutching the top of the truck, sternly asked: " Why then, since you are in uniform, have you no cap? Where is your cap? "

Despite her bleeding leg, the girl also stood up. She was of a lower rank than himself.

" My cap—I left it on—my husband's grave," she said, and suddenly leaned forward, pressed herself to the doctor's body, clutched him, and burst into loud sobs.

He flushed deeply, hesitated, and murmured: " Poor child, forgive me. Take my cap. I will pick one up on my rounds " ; and he placed his own cap on her head. He helped her down from the lorry. We went in together.

" May I report? " the woman called to a sleeping man, the commander.

He awoke with a start, came straight to her, and kissed her on her forehead.

" No need to ; we know everything. Go and have your cry. Tears spoil eyes. It is difficult to take your revenge with bad eyes. Go, Olga. The battle will begin soon."

The woman left the dugout. The lorry in which she had come was now crowded with Marines. They were

lifting the doctor up to a seat on top, in all his dignity as
" Chief of the Immortality Department."

In the dugout the commander turned to me and said:
" Better write this down. A brave beautiful soul—she
was a sapper—lays mines. Before the war she was a
pianist. Thousands of Germans have been killed by mine
fields she has laid. Yesterday she mined the pass they
had chosen for their attack. She worked with her husband. He was wounded. She dragged him out of danger,
killing fifteen Germans on the way, four of them with the
butt of her rifle. She dragged her husband's body over a
mile, dug a grave, and buried him. I would advise you
to write a story about it. No good—just a short note—
looks too much like a fairy-tale."

The commander went to sleep again, and while he slept
I had a look round the dugout, the appearance of which
surprised me. On the walls above the military maps
there were hung curious old-fashioned pictures in moth-
eaten velvet frames. The first one I looked at was called
" Besieged Monastery." It was a romantic battle scene,
the details of which were painted with the precision of a
photograph. From the battlements of their mediæval
monastery the defenders poured molten lead. On the
roof dogs stood barking. The attackers were clambering
up walls or falling into a moat. They had captured the
drawbridge and were using a battering ram on a nail-
studded door. The knight, who was in command of the
attacking force, had his vizor open and was twirling his
moustache at a beautiful lady who was smiling at him
through a tiny window in a tower. Another picture
showed tourists feeding pigeons on the Piazza San Marco,
in Venice ; a third was the portrait of a handsome woman,
with long curling tresses.

On the corner of a table before a cracked mirror lay

portions of a monogrammed silver tea service. The floor was covered with a valuable carpet that had been folded many times. I found out later that all this comfort had belonged to the Hotel London in Odessa. Hating the idea of leaving anything for the Rumanians, the commander had loaded whatever there was room for in a launch and had blown up the rest, including the remainder of the tea service. The comfort, the naïve pictures, the snoring commander, the soft carpet, and the tarnished silver disappointed and surprised me. Here it was quiet and cosy whereas I had been expecting to find the kind of hustle I had grown used to in staff headquarters, where, in nervous laconic phrases, orders were smartly given and executed. But here, only a hundred yards from the Germans, was a man snoring as if at home, a man upon whom much depended. A Red Fleet man entered quietly.

" Is that you, Should-Not-Be-Killed? "

" It is," the sailor answered.

The slumbering commander was heard to say: " Don't you think it's time to wake the Germans up? "

" There is forty minutes yet," the sailor replied.

" All right, give this comrade tea. Give him my portion."

" Your portion it is, Comrade Commander," the sailor replied, and went to the teapot. The commander fell asleep again.

The sailor poured some tea and handed me a mug.

I asked him: " What does that mean—' Should-Not-Be-Killed ' ? "

" That is my name."

" Why that name? "

" A year ago I went to serve on a warship. Of course I was scared, for I had not been under fire before. I used to look for places where shells don't hit. My chief, of

116

course, noticed this and called for me. 'What, are you afraid to die?' 'Yes,' I answered. 'One should not be killed.' 'You told the truth, my smart fellow,' he said to me, and told me that a truthful man always overcomes the fear in himself. He trained me mostly during the coastal raids. Now I am all right. But he keeps using that name for me. Why is he asleep, you ask? Well, comrade writer, you see he hadn't slept for ten days. Yesterday they attacked us eighteen times and we only just pulled through. They haven't many ideas, those Germans, but they keep on pushing, one must admit."

" Is he popular, your commander? "

" After Stalin, he is the man for us."

" Why is he liked? "

" Because he is strong and because he has a heart. You will see for yourself."

The door burst open wide with a crash, and a good-looking young fellow with the proportions of a giant came into the dugout. He was barefooted, his trousers were soaked, and something was wrapped up under his arm. The adjutant stared at him for a moment and then the two sailors flung their arms round each other's necks, thumped each other on the shoulders, and kissed noisily.

The newcomer unwrapped his package. It contained a fish. " Fry it for dinner. I found it stunned on the beach. I guess the chief gets lonesome for a fish like that." He handed over the big slippery, glistening fish, sat down purposefully at a table, and began to write something very fast on the corner of a piece of notepaper:

" I beg you to take me on the land front. I will justify your confidence in me. You will be surprised to see how I will smash those Fascists, Comrade Commander. Sevastopol was, is, and shall be the Black Sea Fleet's main base. Hurrah! " the note ran.

117

" When he wakes up, give him that," said the sailor, getting up.

" Is that you, my excellent one? " asked the chief without opening his eyes.

" It is, Comrade Commander."

" Where did you spring from? "

" From the open sea."

" No joking. How did you manage that without my help? "

" It is true, Comrade Chief, straight out of the sea. Our beauty went down. With my own strength I swam back to you, back to the infantry. For forty-eight hours I clung to planks, cold and wet, with no food. It was dull, too, for after a while all the others had sunk and I was alone. On the third day I got sleepy, twice slipped off the planks, and thought: ' That is enough. I will open my mouth and join my comrades.' And just when I was ready to take the plunge, I saw a boat. I swam towards it. It was ours. They picked me up and here I am."

" Take you long to sink? "

" Two minutes."

" What got you? "

" Two torpedoes."

" Where is my Byron? "

" Sunk."

" A pity. It was a good edition. And, generally speaking, Byron was a decent Englishman. He wrote gentle poetry and died with soldiers. Why have you come back? To boast or to serve? "

" To serve."

" Should-Not-Be-Killed, give him my portion of tea, will you? "

" Yes, your portion, Comrade Chief."

The commander went to sleep again. The adjutant poured the tea and began to clean the fish. The barefoot sailor sipped the hot thick tea with obvious enjoyment.

Suddenly a ship's bell clanged alarmingly. It was the bell from a torpedo boat, which the Marines had brought ashore to remind them, as its deep sound stirred the dugouts into activity, of their true home—the sea.

Several telephones began to ring, and the commander woke up for good.

Before I left the trenches I stayed awhile listening to his commands. He gave them all in strictly naval language as if it were the torpedo boat in which all these men had served and not a sector of the front with its three lines of defence that he was commanding. The staff officers and the commanders of various units had assembled and there began a clamour of sharp orders and rapid consultations.

" What is happening in the stern? Have the artillery wake them up a bit. Make them think we are starting an attack. Fire incessantly."

In precisely two minutes the first shell was fired, then the second and third, and then everything began to rattle and rock. Pictures shook in their velvet frames; tumblers danced on the table. " The stern," which was the farthest sector, was on the telephone line.

" Stern? Louder, speak louder—shout, for God's sake! Please report on the situation."

The chief put the telephone receiver down, turned to a sailor who was writing in the log, and said: " Make entry: ' Stern tells another fairy-tale.' " The chief picked up the receiver again. " Yes, go on, Stern. What? Forty tanks approaching? Why are you sitting there so calmly, then? What, repairing line? Where are the despatch riders? Dig them out. Can you see the tanks clearly? Only too clearly, you say. Is this the first time you have ever seen tanks? Not the first time. Is there anybody standing beside you? Then why are you losing your head in front of your men? Keep steady. A nervous chief is worse than a dead one. Has the number of tanks increased since we began talking? No? And has it decreased? Also no? Strange tanks. How far are they away from the first line? A hundred and thirty yards? You want reinforcements? You know I haven't got any. You are my reinforcements, don't you understand? Adopt anti-tank dispositions. Rapid reforming will strengthen you and weaken the Germans. Take note: ' Forty German tanks divided by a cool-headed two and halved again by common sense gives you ten tanks. Yesterday you damaged fifteen. Today you are lucky.' Good-bye."

" I think that woke him up," the chief said. " Keep an eye on the stern. He is nervous and confused."

An officer saluted and rushed out. As he left, another man burst in.

" Reporting for duty, Comrade Commander."

" And smiling with all sixty-eight teeth, eh? What are you smiling about? Just because a little group of tommy-gunners started a big battle? I see you like battles. Do you dream about Austerlitz? Or do you think there is a big tunnel from Sevastopol to the ' Big Land ' with a conveyor belt bringing us ammunition on it? This isn't a school treat, you know. Shame on you, man. Go back. Your job is not to pound the enemy; it's to beat him. Let him come, Let him come as near as your nerves will stand. Let him come till he is practically stepping on you, and then let him have it. At two hundred yards any fool can hit him. Good-bye. You didn't dig in properly as I told you. Come over afterwards and we'll have some fried fish together."

Other receivers were now off their hooks. The commander took them one by one: " There will be nobody coming from the Tribunal. Use your own judgment. If necessary, shoot them yourself—use tommy guns. We will need our heavies just before the big attack. Yesterday over your sector the German planes flew as low as a hundred and fifty feet. Not everybody is so lucky. But you only got two down by rifle-fire. If that sort of thing goes on again to-day, I shall put you on coast duty. Be stern with them. Headquarters can't give you will-power. Remember. And lead them into battle yourself.

" Is that you, Stern? What! Apologizing? Failure? Only twelve were tanks—the others tractors? Don't be so pleased about it. Twelve tanks constitute danger. Listen, don't try to kid me. You are brave enough in an attack, but you are afraid to speak the truth. No, I am not insulting you. Nobody is insulting you. If you can't be insulted, what the hell are you doing as a commander? Personally you are a brave man, but as a commander you are a liar. Your methods are worth a devil of a lot. Whatever you were forgiven for in peace-time will not be forgiven now—here we pay for mistakes in blood.

" Yesterday, at the Military Soviet, you couldn't say that your task was impossible to fulfil with the numbers of men allotted to you for it. You said yes instead of no because it was harder to say no. You gave the impression of great courage and resolution. Really you were a coward because you hadn't enough strength in you to argue and uphold your point of view. Today you will be killed. That is what happens to men like you. You will be killed because you are not brave enough in conferences. You said that the infantry on the next sector

121

fought badly. Do you know what it means to say that the infantry fought badly? Don't you think it means that the main forces fought badly? And what does it mean when the main forces fight badly? Doesn't it mean that the main forces of the Patriotic War were bad? Isn't that what it means? Damn it all! I saw that in your eyes—that was the only honest thing left in you. The poor women. That is all."

The chief hung up the receiver and then said, as if apologizing: "My commissar has been killed. I have to give orders and explain them now. Did you hear? A lie in war leads straight to death. His life doesn't matter, but his position has got to be held. Send reserves up to his sector, but secretly, so he doesn't know." The commander never raised his voice during these conversations; occasionally he glanced at his watch. It was clear to me that though the conversations were serious enough, they had only secondary importance compared with the events to come. From the way that he did not trouble to look at people when talking to them and the way he yawned and repeated himself, I realized that this man's thoughts had long since been in the battle itself.

He went to the table, looked at a piece of paper a sailor had left there, read it, tore it up, and asked in a grim voice: "Who wrote this?"

"I did," replied a young fellow who was writing in a log, and did not look up as he replied.

"Who told you that we are heroic participants in the defence of Sevastopol?"

"Well, why do the newspapers say so?"

"Newspapers? When we have been dead a hundred years, my honourable friend, then it will be decided with the utmost precision what we are. History apportions credit and puts it in its order of merit, not the staff officers and the journalists. You have gone rather too far in writing about yourself, for that is what it means—'I am a hero of the defence of Sevastopol.' For that you deserve to be nailed to a mast upside down. Prepare an order to forbid such uncouth expressions as 'Germans leaked through,' 'We are surrounded,' 'Heroic Sevastopol,' 'Drunken enemy,' and other such nonsense, and forbid their being spoken even in a state of intoxication. Do you understand, heroic clerk? "

"Yes, sir."

"Then let us go to the trenches."

We left the dugout. The guns had finished firing. The silence was abrupt and unexpected. In the nearest trench a gramophone was playing. There was loud and infectious laughter, laughter from the never despondent but buoyant heart of the Russian. The tune was popular among the men, who, like their commanders, had not slept for days, for in this time of the defence no one was relieved and no one thought or talked of rest.

"Wonder what they are playing now," a sailor asked the commissar, pausing a moment to try and catch the tune. "*Katiusha* was broken yesterday. It's a pity. It was a good record. Someone left it under the gun carriage and forgot to cover it with his cap. Listen a minute. Yes, that is what it is, of course. It is Heinkel singing."

"Not Heinkel—Henkkin," corrected the commissar.

"What are you talking about? " the commander asked. "Better get a move on. See, the Germans are quieter. Now they will attack."

At this moment something remarkable happened in the enemy trenches, the like of which had never happened before on the Sevastopol front. It was solemn religious chanting that reached our ears from the enemy lines, a great chorus that surged across the bitter, stony ground.

123

The gramophone was stopped and everybody listened. It was the Rumanians, praying for victory, despairingly, as they faced the sun on the Crimean hills.

"It is a jolly religion they have, Comrade Political Commissar," said a soldier as he sorted his reserve cartridge boxes. Only minutes now remained before the battle would begin. All awaited the appearance of the bombers. The trenches became livelier. The awakening sailors rubbed their stubbly cheeks with heavy hands and washed their eyes carefully with water poured from mugs into their cupped hands. They had to be careful about water, for there was little. Out of holes in the rocky sides of the trenches they produced bread and tobacco. As they smoked they looked about them, considering the appearance of the sky and the enemy trenches.

The men maintained order in the front-line positions, which were as trim as their quarters on board ship. In little niches carved from the rock, they stored water and bullets, for at this time the strictest economy in both was necessary. They would lend bullets to one another, keeping careful calculations. Those who were in debt would shoot rarely, realizing what it would mean to waste ammunition.

I went towards the right flank, a well-fortified height which was nearer to Belbek. If need be, I could get away from here fairly easily and, what was more important, I would have a commanding view of the battlefield.

Room is made for me in the sheltered camouflaged command point. Inside this dugout, binoculars in hand and close to a telephone, the commander stands. With him are his bare-foot sailor, his adjutant, and several assistants. The eyes of all are fixed on the narrow sector between two valleys, where the battle is to take place.

Our side is defended by three lines of trenches and a

very complicated system of mine fields and gun positions. Here, as in all four sectors of the Sevastopol defences, control is centralized. The day is windless. There is a strange unpleasant atmosphere before this attack. Never before has there been a German attack without a prelude of hundreds of tons of shells being pumped into our positions. Perhaps the Germans are exhausted? Perhaps this is the end of the third offensive? Then why all these preparations for an attack? Perhaps they are only a cover to give their men a rest.

I hear the chief's voice: " Zero hour. Ready for the fireworks," and at the same moment I see tanks creeping out from the left side of the valley. They are followed by running figures. Through my glasses I can distinguish faces. They are half naked and really do look drunk. They have the butts of their tommy guns pressed against their sweating bodies. Only the officers are in full uniform. They have cotton in their nostrils because of the stench of the corpses. Why is it so quiet? Oh, to smash, to smash, to tear, to choke, to kill them! Why so quiet? They are drawing near. Some, I see, carry movie cameras recording the battle.

The air is rent by the piercing sound of trumpets, which are decorated with regimental flags and are carried by the Rumanians and the Germans, who run boldly towards our front lines. The tanks come on and then suddenly stop. The chief picks up a telephone. " Fire all calibres without ceasing. Stop only if directly dive-bombed. Armour-breakers to advance. Fifth unit to separate German infantry from tanks. Machine-gun fire to be held."

Everything is enveloped in smoke. Nothing is visible. Into this dusty fog we shoot. Dust and smoke clouds can hang over a battlefield for days, and for days, too, the guns will pour their shot into it, aiming blindly. Someone reminds me that this is the twelfth day of the battle. It is strange, but I am not excited. It may be because I am not participating or because the tension has quite surpassed reality. I leave the shelter and return to have a look at our neighbouring positions, all the while keeping a check on the Marines' sector through my binoculars.

Hours pass. The battle rages. It is still working up to its climax. Now tanks are occasionally breaking through the pall of smoke and nearing our lines. It is practically impossible to recognize them. Pieces of glass sparkle in the sun as bottles are smashed against the sides of turrets and fire spurts from the caterpillars. The weight of the explosions presses down on one's head, squeezing brain, eyes, and ear-drums until it seems as though one can bear no more and that one's head will be battered into shapelessness.

The leading tanks have reached the trenches. Somehow they are checked there and the next wave passes them by. Suddenly they wheel sharply, scrunching the bodies of German and Rumanian soldiers who have just been killed in the assault. Several of our batteries have received direct hits and are silenced. This allows six more tanks to break through to the trenches. They are met with armour-piercing bullets—thermite-tipped bullets which burn their way through toughened steel and fill the inside of the tanks with inflammable vapour. The tank men jump out and the sailors shoot them. But despite our veil of deadly fire, the enemy prevails.

More tanks are moving up to replace the blackened hulks of those burned out. Four more drive into our positions. Close behind them are Rumanian and German infantrymen. I see tanks swing around as they meet our fire and crush their own men or cause them to scatter and expose themselves to our rifle-fire. Two more tanks are at our trenches. The tongues of flame which dart from their sides lick our dugouts and earthworks. Their fire splashes lightly over the rocks. Still more tanks emerge from the sides of the valley, with numerous infantry, so that the whole sector seems crowded with machines. The men are piling up like lava, gradually but inexorably, against our positions which are not yet pierced. The fire of our long-range and field artillery is incessant. From where I stand I can see the battery of Malakhov Kurgan.

The latest tanks to enter the battle move fast, zig-zagging cleverly to use the cover of the damaged and abandoned machines. The infantry, too, dash from one position to another. Then the Marines go in to counter-attack. I see them bound forward in that first thrilling moment of the battle, leap over the parapet, and thrust towards the enemy. Hundreds of men in white and blue striped jerseys, loudly cursing the enemy and his creator, are engaging the Rumanians on the left flank. Hand-to-hand fighting comes as a relief after the fiendish tension of machine warfare. The enemy is scattered and retires.

The commander, within whose sight all this has been taking place, is prudent. He orders his men to fall back, and the thinning ranks of the Marines return to their trenches. Then come the bombers. Today is the fourth day that the battle for this tortured piece of ground has continued. The Germans decide to strike decisively from the air. An air battle is in progress above the bombers now, with our planes outnumbered eight or ten to one. Wrecked machines crash on the battlefield, destroying tanks and men as their own bombs explode.

These German and Italian dive-bombers are attacking a two-hundred-yard sector of our front lines. It is not a battle but an execution, a complete overwhelming of the earth and the men on it, and when the planes have swept on, enemy tanks and infantry pick their way through the craters that are left. Those who defended the second line saw everything that happened ; they saw their comrades wiped out and smashed, but they stood firm. No one ran away.

The bombers silence our artillery. They dive-bomb our anti-aircraft guns, our heavy guns, field guns, machine guns—everything that is there. The enemy's object is to advance from the first to the second lines. In separate patches of trenches our men, having been enveloped in the waves of advancing enemy and cut off from their base by craters, continue to fight. It is a hopeless battle for those remnants of the first-line troops, but the men who hold the second line and have watched it know that it is a battle that has to be fought, and can be fought, and that it is remorselessly approaching them.

Now about one hundred planes are over our positions, swooping in precise dives. They operate almost unpunished. Each one in a chain aims its bombs to fall beside those of the one which dived before it.

Gradually the German tanks and infantry emerge from the cover of craters they have captured, and assume formation for an assault on our second line. Their long-range artillery and monster mortars are now in action. Night has long since fallen. The dive-bombers are shifted along the line to tackle a new sector. The enemy's infantry and tanks are extending their menacing concentration. Everything indicates the imminence of a break-through. Having forced a wedge in our first line, if they can muster enough force to break our stubbornness in about twenty minutes of fighting, they can reach the road leading to Sevastopol.

I cannot deny that all of us at the command point believed that the enemy would succeed in breaking through. He had absolute mastery of the air. In such circumstances continued resistance on our first line was not enough—words were not enough. Taking his revolver from its holster, the commander left the dugout, telling all to remain at their posts, then ran down the hill and out of sight.

Again the German and Rumanian infantry came in to attack, again the bombers zoomed over our lines, again the tanks advanced. For more than two hours the battle raged, and during that time the enemy forced our three lines in depth, and into our flank, so that in some places we held a belt of ground not wider than thirty yards. Two or three more spasms and he would be clear through.

Darkness and smoke threw a pall over the battle line, but by the crescendo of bursting shells and bombs I could sense the Germans' approach to the road. It was time to abandon my trench and I was preparing to leave when suddenly the gunfire ceased. Someone came to me and said: "They have paused—waiting for reserves. Our commander has been killed. Do you care to come and help bury him?" As I picked my way down the hillside, clutching the hand of someone who led me into the unknown, into a place of smoke, fire, screams, and oaths, he told me how the commander had died.

When we had lost all our guns, when scarcely a man remained alive in the sector and the Germans were aware of the gap before them leading straight to the road, our commander found one anti-aircraft gun intact. He gathered together a skeleton crew, adjusted the gun, and began point-blank fire on the enemy, which lasted a quarter of an hour.

It was enough to make the enemy think that we had received reinforcements, and he paused for his own reserves to reach him, in perhaps only a matter of a few minutes. We reached a dugout which was intact except for four gaping craters around it, so that now instead of being underground it stood on a little eminence. Beside a smashed gun lay our commander. There was blood on him. Sailors knelt beside him. Some of them were crying. Some were pressing their jerseys to his wounds so that they could carry his blood on their clothes.

Should-Not-Be-Killed drew his hand from his pocket and placed it on his chief's breast, saying: " Give what you can, men. We will pay for a tank as a memorial. Do you understand? " The sailors took money carefully from their leather purses and laid it on the body until the commander's breast and hands were covered with notes.

And then, at this precise tense moment, the commander stirred and said: " What kind of pay is this, may I ask? Get me a surgeon and the major, quickly." We carried the wounded man into the dugout, laid him on a plank, and while we waited for the surgeon, whom nobody could find, we washed him. He was severely wounded. The major arrived. Turning towards him, the commander said: " Isn't it your impression, major, that after you got your first medal you began to fight worse? "

" No," said the major, who was extraordinarily vain.

A girl came in. She was the one with whom I had travelled on the previous day. She looked at the commander's leg. " It will have to be cut off."

" Can it be done tomorrow? " the wounded man asked.

" Yes, it can wait till tomorrow."

She left and the commander went on talking with the major.

"Don't be shy, major. The same thing happened to me. With my first decoration I thought I had won immortality and the right to watch others being brave in the future. I felt sure I had won the right to remain alive, and that it was the duty of those who had no decorations to die. I thought that henceforth I had the right to stop being brave and risking my life. No, don't be embarrassed, major. Lead the men to attack right away and I bet you that the second time you do it you will have lost every scrap of fear."

The major was a dandy. Even in this battle he had, somehow, managed to keep his boots clean.

"Is that advice or an order?"

"Both," replied the commander.

"Well, I will think about the advice after I have fulfilled the order, Comrade Commander."

"Very good," said the commander, and he fell asleep. The major left.

Should-Not-Be-Killed began at last to fry his fish and took a portion of it over to the captain.

"Tomorrow," he said, "after they have operated." And he fell asleep again.

In the morning the commander lost his leg, a member of the Military Soviet arrived and awarded the major a second decoration, and the Germans resumed their attack.

CHAPTER XI

ONE night I was aroused and asked to go immediately to see a member of the Military Council. On my way to his room I noticed that during the two hours I had been sleeping everything at the Admiralty had changed remarkably. Radio operators were carrying their equipment on their shoulders. Mechanics were ripping wires from walls and throwing telephones out of the rooms. The chief of administration was smashing mirrors in the barber shop by wielding an electric fan in a most ruthless manner. An officer on staff duty was using a rifle butt to smash typewriters. With a cigarette in his mouth, a Marine was dragging a sack of explosives into the engine room. In every room people were burning documents. Acrid smoke spread through all the corridors. The chief of transport sat with his feet on a table humming his favourite song, " Open wide the gates," which meant that he was ready to see the last ships off from Sevastopol. Over his head there had been written in charcoal on the wall: " *No pasarán.*"* A waiter was helping the chief of the decorations staff to pack the medals which had not been given out.

To my surprise, there was no trace of hurry in all these actions. On the contrary, in everything going on around me I noticed a desire to work as slowly as possible, thoroughly and methodically to destroy everything that could be destroyed.

Those who were not engaged in the demolition and the transfer of the Admiralty to the new place, which had been necessitated by a German break-through on the North Side, carried on with their usual duties. When I

* " They shall not pass !"   (Spanish.)

132

saw the commissar, calculating on his counting frame the amount of explosives required to destroy the Admiralty's present headquarters, I had no doubts about what was happening and entered the room of the member of the Military Soviet with complete understanding. Here everything was as before—everything except the flags. The little red flags which had marked positions on the Sevastopol map were lying on a plate. The member of the Military Soviet was sitting in an armchair—not, as usual, at his table. His attitude implied clearly that his work was finished and that there was no longer any point in sitting at his desk. He greeted me quietly with his unshakable good humour and told me: " I am sorry, but the psychological moment for your departure has come. All such patriotic exclamations as ' I can't leave you in such difficult circumstances,' or ' As a party member I must die,' are quite beside the point. You weren't sent here to die. I don't believe in editors who boast about the number of their correspondents who have been killed. You are supposed to write about the war on the Black Sea coast. If you do, we will be grateful. Eighteen days in Sevastopol is something for you nervous people. Sorry—our nerves have become wires. Nothing surprises us now. But you are a writer. You must still be a little surprised, and while you still feel like that, write. I used to write at school—poetry. It was rather bad—no, very bad. Go back on a submarine. The commissar will take you to Streletskaya Harbour with the chief of transport. You know him, I believe. No need to give you any advice. You may have trouble on the way, or maybe you will not be noticed. Don't give up your uniform. Take it. It is your present—Sevastopol uniform. Good-bye. I think we shall meet again. Anything may happen."

133

He had no time for conversation. That I could see. I said: "Good-bye," and left as quickly as possible.

In the waiting-room a captain approached me. He was a man I had met in the mess. "I hear you are leaving," he said. "Would you be so kind as to take a letter to my wife in Moscow? My home in Sokolniki is called Sailors' Rest just as in Chekhov. It is a bungalow."

While I was wrapping up in a naval raincoat my files of Sevastopol newspapers, notes, pamphlets, and books picked up in the ruins of the Panorama, the captain sat at a table and finished his letter. Neither of us had an envelope, so he handed me a page covered with bold script and said: "It doesn't matter. What secrets can there be now? You will put it in an envelope when you reach the 'Big Land.' It is very short and is not what I meant to say, but how can one write it? I should like you to take the letter personally and try to explain everything."

"What is there to explain?" I asked.

"We are abandoning Sevastopol," the captain answered, gripping my hand between both of his and shaking it strongly. I then left quickly.

Since then I have read the letter.

Yes, Anka, we shall not see each other. An hour ago I was called and told: "We trust you to die here. You will do this job and you will not get back alive. We are not trying to frighten you, but don't deceive yourself. The wounded are being withdrawn to Chersonese. Cover them—until the last man, the last yard, the last breath. Some one of us will be with you. Whom we shall decide now. You may refuse. We shall not shoot you. You

134

have behaved here very well." I was deadly silent. I wanted to refuse, but could not. Suddenly, just as before the attack, my thoughts became disturbed, and for the first time I began to consider what was going to happen to me, and how. But however hard I thought, it did not help me to find the place and hour of my death or to recognize the hand of my executioner. That meant I was healthy. That was a wise man who said : " Ignorance is the best drug before dying." But I know, and I am going. I am not a hero and you know it, Anka. Death never stood very close to me before. I was promised life. Why and for what reason am I doing this ? And while waiting for my regiment and looking into my seething mind I find the answer. Here in this war the most splendid deeds are done not only because men are great in spirit but because they have learned to obey automatically, and that is a great force. From discipline to heroism is only one step. And if we talk about our idea of a fighter, first of all we have got to consider him as one who fulfils orders. One who understands that he is being true to the principles of our country. Damn it, we can't even die without philosophizing. When I said : " Yes, General," this former officer in the Czar's Army came to me and, patting me on the shoulder, said : " We didn't order you, because in these times it is important that a man should order himself. There are Germans who go to their death as consciously as you. There are ! And they do it quite well, sometimes better than we. But that is not heroism, just gangster pride. Your deed is heroic because you will die in the defence of your soil while they die trying to conquer territory. I congratulate you. I know that you will do this job. Take my medal. Old medals suit youngsters."

I refused, but the sixty-two-year-old general took his

Red Banner Order, kissed it according to Old Guard tradition, and gave it to me with the words: " Make ready, Captain. I shall be with you."

I am telling you everything just as it was said to me. It is better so as to make it clean-cut and not torture your life with vain hopes and senseless guessing. How foolish that we had no children! Life should continue. For its continuation we die the best way we can. It would have been a thousand times easier for me if there were growing up beside you a true heir to my spirit and the feelings of my heart. A dying man has got to see succession. Then death is as reasonable as birth. My dear, I would not have given you to anyone. Husbands who give up their wives are scoundrels. When we loved we were sparing in words. Now it is too late. There is no use to talk. I know you love me. Wait for me. I know that when I am dead, for you I will continue to live, and that nobody will oust me from your heart. I know this wound will never heal. But if it happens that you meet a man fine enough for your grief whom you will love a little, and if as the result of your love you have a new life and it is a son, then let him bear my name. Let him be my continuation, though I am dead and your new friend is alive. This would not punish him, for not everybody must die and if he cannot understand and would not like it, then leave him without sorrow or tears or longings and let it be not his but our son; and when a new Sevastopol is built, come here, and somewhere on Chersonese, somewhere near the sea, plant poppies. They grow here very well. And that will be my grave. It may be that you will make a mistake. Maybe it won't be me but another who lies there. It doesn't matter. Someone else will think of her own and plant flowers above me. Nobody will be left out, for we shall lie close and there will be no space to spare where we lie.

Farewell. I am glad they warned me about death. Otherwise I would not have talked to you—my joy, my blood, my life. I love you. I love you till the last drop of my blood. . . .

The lights failed. The commissar came in carrying a candlestick. "Let's go," he said. It was dark in the corridors. A long line of candles stretched far away, throwing a dim light on the walls. For the first time I noticed that they glistened with damp. Somewhere through the crushed rock above, water was filtering. Bombs had done that. At the entrance somebody from a ship insistently announced: "Last ship from Sevastopol leaving. Last ship from Sevastopol. Whoever has a pass for the 'Big Land,' hurry up."

During our long walk through labyrinthine passages in the rock, the phrase persistently followed us—"Last ship from Sevastopol leaving."

We came out of the dugout, got in a car, and drove up the mountain. As we left the city, there moved on us from three sides nervously twinkling and shifting red lights. German shock troops. The chief of transport took out a useful-looking revolver, gave me some grenades, and, leaning towards his chauffeur, shouted: "Come on, Jora, as fast as you can."

The car jerked ahead. The red lights moved swiftly upon us. There were many of them. The chief of transport climbed on to the running board and, shooting as he spoke, cried out: "Pif—paf, dies the little Hänschen, right away."

"Lie down," he told me. I heard shots. The red lights were now behind us. We had broken through.

137

" On my way back it will be worse," said the chief of transport, " and next time still worse," and he climbed back into the car.

The fourth sector of defence extended from a State farm which was named after Sophia Perovskaya to the village of Belbek. Before the Revolution the farm was Perovsky's estate. It was just in that part of the sector that the Germans came out on the North Side; they had come out, but had not broken through. For once they met with practically no resistance. There was no carelessness or treachery—nobody ran away or surrendered. The reason was simply this: there was nobody left alive there to stop them. It was a victory over the dead. Out of the division that had been defending that part of the line only 130 men were left. Entire regiments had been wiped out. After fulfilling their last duties there, the soldiers lay at peace among the havoc of wrecked dugouts and crumbled trenches.

The Germans did not believe that they were dead. They were suspicious and fearful of the corpses. Stabbing and slashing the bodies with their bayonets or emptying their revolvers into them, they sneaked forward under the cover of light tanks towards the Konstantinovsky Battery.

Immediate capture of this battery, which was famous for the stubbornness with which it had defended itself during the Crimean War, would have given the enemy complete possession of the North Side and control of the entrance to the bay, the town, the harbour, and the channel to the sea.

The 130 survivors had long since received an order to abandon their positions. They ignored it, rejecting their chance of safety. They chose their narrowest sector and made ready for its defence. Commanded by a major, the only major left in the division, this handful of men fought on their last line of defence and fought so resolutely that the line could not be pierced and the Germans were checked and forced to pause for reinforcements. These 130 men, who had been assembled hastily on the field of battle, fought for the lives of their wounded comrades who were being carried to the beaches to be ferried across the bay. Their stubborn defence prolonged the life of the city itself and caused many more Germans to perish in its capture.

There were women working beside the Marines. All but two had been decorated for bravery in previous battles —doctors and nurses who, during the eight months of siege, had saved thousands of soldiers. They were mostly young women; some were mere girls, whose bravery had astonished the men. Now under German bullets, shrapnel, and high explosives, scratched and bruised by stones and earth that had been flung from craters, they were bearing away the wounded to Konstantinovsky Battery and to the landing-places.

The wounded, many of them horribly mauled about, lay along the beaches—800 of them. The supplies of iodine, drugs, bandages, bread and water had long since been exhausted or destroyed—there was literally nothing to ease their distress or to make the task of those who succoured them any lighter. Everyone knew this—the doctors and the wounded. There were no reproaches, no complaints. The wounded suffered and died quietly. Young Russian women who had served in the Army from the beginning of the war, and who thought themselves lucky when posted at the Sevastopol front, now screened with their bodies the wounded from splinters of bombs and shells, found shelter for them in caves along the rocky coast, carried them to boats, and sank or swam with them when their boat was hit.

The men who were fighting that all this might go on, those 130, knew what the women were doing. They knew that they were getting their comrades away to safety. And they fought with an unslackening courage. Even when reinforcements arrived the Germans were still unable to break through this last but most stubbornly defended line of defence. But the ranks of the Marines thinned rapidly and it was a mere forty who made the last stand at Konstantinovsky Battery.

For three days and three nights forty men held that battery—days and nights when the German attack was incessant. For three days and nights these sailors closed the gates to Sevastopol, and only when all their ammunition had been spent did the survivors swim across the bay to the South Side. The last to plunge into the water was the wounded major, and with his departure resistance on the fourth sector of the Sevastopol defence ended.

Once they were in possession of the North Side, the Germans turned their attention to the famous coastal battery of twelve-inch naval guns which covered the approaches to Sevastopol from this side. For several days the guns of this huge underground fortress had been silent. It had been bombed by the Germans. Twenty Stukas had dived and rained their bombs on its steel turret. The steel held, but the crew which had defended the now distorted guns was ordered to evacuate, to leave for the South Side. It could have been done then, but the answer came back proudly over the air: " We will die on our own soil."

After the German infantry had reached the battery, the Admiralty Headquarters began to receive messages every half-hour: " We are forty-six."—" The Germans are knocking on the turrets and asking us to surrender. Twice we have opened the hatchway to throw grenades at them. Now it is impossible to get out. There are too many of them."—" They have put wood around the battery, smoke is leaking through, they are trying to choke us."—" We are thirty-seven."—" Thirty left."—" Twenty-eight."— " Twenty-two."—" We are now preparing to blow ourselves up."—" Am now ceasing transmission. Farewell." Shortly afterwards the battery blew up with the most shattering of all the explosions of Sevastopol.

The German tommy-gunners in the meanwhile were crossing the bay on rubber boats towards the South Side. The Admiralty, however, did not quit its underground headquarters although the enemy now had his guns trained directly on the entrance, placing the group which was working there, under the direct command of the Red Fleet, in the most acute danger of being imprisoned in the caverns. Headquarters was not abandoned because the Sevastopol garrison still presented a front to the enemy and, although retreating slowly, did not allow itself to become disintegrated, with a consequent inevitable break-through into the town. It was essential that control of the front with its scattered units, the operations of which needed to be exactly dovetailed into the coastal anti-aircraft defence, should remain centralized in a single headquarters whence contact could still be maintained by the few remaining telephone cables and by radio.

And so, from within the rock below the city it continued to direct operations and give orders calmly, orders which often were terrible in their implication. Nobody went out into the fresh air, and the mess room was deserted, for there was little to eat. The inmates grew thin and yellow. It was evident to all that they were staring death in the face, since there was no way out.

Finally it was decided to try to blast a way through the roof of the cave, since by this time the entrance was dominated by German guns. It was reasoned that should the force of the explosion kill them all, at any rate it would be better than surrender, while if a way through the rock was forced, the commander of Sevastopol would be able to reach the town and continue to direct its defence.

The most remote room was chosen for the attempt, and cases of explosives were carried along the dark and stuffy corridors of the rock. It took a long time to arrange them and there was much argument over how it would be best to carry out the operation. Finally everyone sought safety as far away from the place as possible.

I am not qualified to describe that explosion. I was not there and did not hear it. But survivors have told me that it was as successful as so dangerous an operation could be expected to be. Extricating themselves from the ruins of their headquarters and clambering over shattered rock to escape from the collapse which threatened to occur at any moment, the survivors broke through the fumes and flame, and, by helping each other as they went, supporting the wounded, choking and singed, they finally emerged into the city and made for the Thirty-fifth Battery, which henceforth became the command point for the further defence of Sevastopol.

This manœuvre soon became known to the enemy, who had assumed that he had the Russian High Command trapped and had already reported this by telegram. His reaction was immediate. New forces were accumulated from all over the Crimean Peninsula. Kerch was denuded. And with these reinforcements a new attack was launched in the central sector, with the object of dividing the Balaklava and Chersonese groups from the main force

142

which was defending the central front and was now withdrawing, although in good order and fighting back hard.

The defenders were short of every kind of ammunition and were sorely lacking in men. Their position had reached its gravest moment—Sevastopol faced its most grim ordeal. The question that all in command asked themselves was whether it was possible for the defenders, who were short of water, medical supplies, shells and ammunition, to continue to fight. Would not the men stretch their sunburned arms towards the blue sky and pray to God for mercy? It was not so. During those last hours the men of Sevastopol surpassed themselves in courage; they were fantastic and magnificent in their fearlessness. They had no illusions about their peril but faced death calmly.

Gathering around him the Marines of Captain Alexander's Thirty-fifth Battery on Malakhov Kurgan, the political commissar spoke as follows: " I know that every one of you would rather fight one hundred desperate battles on the sea than be dive-bombed once on shore. But the Germans have forced us to fight on shore. Eighty-two years ago a Russian admiral ordered his men to sink their vessels in this Sevastopol Bay. These orders were obeyed and their guns were brought ashore to defend the city as these our guns are doing today. Twenty-four years ago Lenin ordered our ships to be sunk at Novorossiisk. Those orders were obeyed. Last year Stalin ordered us to blow up the Dnieper Dam and we did. Now we have to die. We have to die for those who one day will return to Sevastopol. We have to die for those who will one day build another Dnieper Dam. We have to die for those who will go on fighting at sea."

The men removed their caps and stood silent for a short time. Then they swore their oath to Stalin and their Fatherland to conquer or die. They returned to their guns wearing under Red Army blouses their striped sailor jerseys—" for luck "—and twisted around their forage caps hat-bands bearing the names of their former ships.

By now the air attack had reached its climax. New planes were being thrown in by the hundred. Over the city, over the port, and over its approaches they hung like a cowl of death, beneath which the enemy reckoned that Sevastopol would choke for lack of food, water, munitions, bandages, fuel, reinforcements—everything essential for a continued defence. For a long time he had expected a white flag of capitulation.

The Germans were unable to divide the army of Sevastopol and smash it group by group, as was their plan. Sevastopol continued to fight back. Over the dead, still sea the moon shone, treacherously robbing the defenders of their hope that the fleet might bring them some last-minute help. The surface of the water, in those days at the turn of the month and the beginning of July, showed how perilous the sea had become. Huge spreading oil stains, protruding masts of perished transports, wreckage of submarines and German planes, drifting lifebelts, furniture, and corpses told of the battle going on.

At last Inkerman fell after concentrated dive-bombing. By then it was clear to everybody that Sevastopol's days were numbered. Nobody deluded himself into thinking otherwise. We knew that this was the beginning of the end. Our mood became grim and angry. The issue was clear and every man steeled himself to extreme ruthlessness. It did not seem that anyone considered we had been defeated. There was never any discussion about a possible capitulation. The battle just went on. It was a terrible battle which became more violent and desperate even when its crisis had passed and the result was apparent.

Before the enemy's relentless steam-roller advance, Sevastopol itself—for now Sevastopol had ceased to be a city and had become a cause which its defenders bore with them, and a tradition which had winged its way to all Russia—fell back with those tortured, sweating, bleeding, swearing sailors who, step by step, with their breasts to the enemy, retreated towards the last lighthouse in Crimea—the Chersonese.

Not one battery fell into the enemy's hands. One by one, as they exhausted their ammunition or were disabled, they blew themselves up. Only for the wounded was there a way out. On cars, stripped of tyres and clattering along on their rims, on gun carriages, in the arms of their comrades, they were taken down to the sea and under fire put in sea planes, submarines, or barges and taken to the " Big Land." As they lay on beaches with tears streaming down their faces, they bade farewell to those who stayed behind.

German military experts were astonished, not so much at the stubbornness of our troops defending Sevastopol in those last days as at the astonishing harmony in the co-ordination of all our various units. In the gradual retreat the men of Sevastopol performed brilliant feats of arms, and round the glorious banners they carried with them won fame for their skill as well as their courage. At the approaches to Sevastopol there disappeared once and for ever the infantryman's fear of tanks, on which the Germans had based their tactics in so many other sectors of the war.

The Black Sea Fleet, which was practically without aircraft protection, proved during those eight long months that the German contention that their blockade would bring the city to its knees in the second month was an idle boast. On the hills of the Crimea the Red Fleet's coastal batteries added glory to the great history of Russian artillery. The men of Sevastopol had shown the Germans at the walls and among the ruins of their city that the Red Army does not surrender, even when at bay in the most hopeless circumstances.

For eight months this town, which was not a very large place and had been built and fortified to withstand attack from the sea, had stemmed the advance of the whole German and Rumanian Crimean army.

Now we were leaving this town and these ruins. Through demolished streets were coming the survivors, many of them wounded, of the staff of the Black Sea Fleet. Slowly the front was sagging and its valiant defenders falling back among the rubble, the avalanches of shattered bricks, piles of masonry, twisted girders, and festoons of broken cables, towards the Chersonese Peninsula. It was reckoned that at that time only eleven buildings in Sevastopol remained intact.

In these tragic, arduous moments a series of conferences was called. Each military or naval unit sent six representatives to the rear, later to report to all a brief but frank explanation of the position. They were told at these meetings that the aim of the battle which still lay ahead, but which all knew was the last, was the slaughter of the greatest possible number of the enemy. They were told that only the wounded would leave the peninsula, and they swore that henceforth they would sell their lives for the highest possible number of enemy killed. Nobody mentioned the possibility of an eventual evacuation—that was not even hinted at. At one of the conferences a sailor asked the commissar: " It is true, Comrade Commander, that the British surrendered at Singapore and Tobruk? "

146

The commissar, who had never before lied to his men, did not at once reply and then answered: " No. It is wrong and a lie."

The end had now come. In the heart of the dense pall of dust and smoke that had masked Sevastopol during the past week, gigantic explosions were taking place. Everything that could not be taken away was blown up. Even damaged guns were pushed into the sea to prevent the enemy from using them for scrap. Horses were shackled and drowned, or killed by grenades in the fields.

Already the Germans had reached the town cemetery and had begun executions of the few civilians who fell into their hands. From his hide-out the traitor Vasily Nikitin came to meet the enemy, and two hours after the German vanguard had entered the town this wily chauffeur, who had several times been convicted for crime, and who was a notorious evil liver and a good-for-nothing, was appointed Burgomaster.

The moon shone treacherously as before. Long before they had reached Sevastopol, every one of our ships became a target for dive-bombing and torpedo-carrying planes, by night as well as by day. Losses during their assistance to Sevastopol were inevitable. Judged by any ordinary standard, a decision to risk them would be considered criminally reckless, and all understood that— those who waited on the beaches and those who were on the sea straining every sinew to reach them. Both groups thought that safety was out of reach, both considered that they were condemned to die. In this lies the essence of Sevastopol's heroic tragedy—to bring help which might not avail, men had to die and died willingly, as willingly as those who knew that help could never reach them, that safety was out of their grasp.

The Last Days

Step by step, in dense ranks, the men of Sevastopol slowly retreated, covering the evacuation of those who had to leave for the " Big Land." It was no strict military formation that held off the enemy, yet it was orderly. In that glorious company were sailors, gunners, cavalrymen, pilots, couriers, infantrymen, women, and youths. It was the most severe test of character that anyone in Sevastopol had to face during the eight months of siege. Everyone in that rear guard had to fight with a single aim —that of getting as much ammunition as possible and selling his life at the highest price. They were swept to a pitch of exaltation that has been rarely known in the history of war. Dying sailors dipped their fingers in blood and wrote on the earth in feeble characters " Return to Sevastopol." Those who were able to leave Sevastopol that last day because of the rear guard's indomitable courage will come back, and not alone. With them will come all who associate with the word " Sevastopol " pride of man in himself, his love for the Fatherland, his devotion to the lofty principles of our country, his regard for its history, and his faith in its future. On that last day the behaviour of the rear guard wrote the most glorious page in all Sevastopol's story.

Could their nerves stand the strain? How would they behave, those who stayed to defend the last strip of Crimean soil and gave the opportunity for most of the civilians and the many wounded to leave? How would they behave? What would they say when they saw the sea without ships? Would they not curse their fathers and their destiny, which in this heavy moment had left them to face the implacable enemy alone, with their backs to the sea? Would the last pages of the history of Sevasstopol be smirched by a panic of desperation—a final breakdown in face of death? That was not the way the people of Sevastopol chose. I saw wounded who did not want to leave. I saw them sobbing, with their faces on the beaches, pressing their bodies against stones, kissing the sand and hugging their beloved earth. I heard them imploring not to be taken away from Sevastopol, begging the right to be left to die beside their comrades who, by the order of the High Command, stayed to cover the evacuation of the garrison. It was not without difficulty that these wounded men were torn from the earth of Sevastopol, and as, finally, they were borne to ships or submarines, or were taken into crowded sea-planes, many of them clutched in their hands pebbles or sand " of Sevastopol."

There were others who behaved differently. Few, very few. These ran with maddened eyes, with tunics torn and flopping, panic-stricken, bewildered, miserable, frightened people. They seized feverishly any kind of craft they could find—rafts, rubber floats, automobile tyres—and flung themselves into the sea. Nobody harmed them. " Let them go their way," the men of the rear guard muttered as they chose positions for their last battle.

There were scoundrels, too, who appeared with bandages on the jetties and asked to be evacuated before the others. They were unbandaged and their lies exposed. By silent agreement of all honest men, they were summarily shot as cowards and traitors. They were monsters and deserved such a death.

Meanwhile the last regiments of the Sevastopol defence were dying like heroes, but killing hundreds of the enemy. Forced to the sea, they continued to fire their automatics until they ran out of ammunition. Then they hurled their rifles away, and swam until they were drowned. Two groups fought their way through Balaklava to join partisans in the Crimean hills, and more will be heard of these.

Behind the Chersonese Lighthouse a new line of defence was re-established. The Thirty-fifth Battery remained active. The local airfield was held to the last. Planes, cutters, submarines, and barges were in contact with the Chersonese Peninsula until the fourth week of July, though officially our troops abandoned the Sevastopol sector on July 3.

Only on the 14th did the group of sailors who were resisting at the Chersonese Lighthouse cease fire. Even the Germans admitted that the fighting had continued eleven days after the official Soviet date of Sevastopol's abandonment.

With every means at their disposal, the Black Sea Flotilla sought to evacuate the wounded from this tip of the Crimean coast where resistance was continuing. At a port on the eastern coast of the Black Sea I watched a cutter land which had left Sevastopol on July 10. It was the *Papanin*. She was mastless, her bridge had been shot away, and her sides were riddled like a sieve, but the Germans had not managed to sink her. The first words of the weary, battle-stained and wounded sailors on reaching land were: "We shall return to Sevastopol. We have seen how the lamps of the Chersonese Lighthouse went out, but we shall light them again." I noticed among these wounded sailors one who was wearing a curious old-fashioned large button alongside his medals.

"What is that button?" I asked.

"It is Admiral Nakhimov's. They bombed the museum and we found his torn uniform. We took the buttons to wear in memory of Sevastopol."